The Loneliness Cure

A Guide to Contentment

I trust this book finds the perfect reader!

Dianne A Allen

Dianne A. Allen, MA

BALBOA
PRESS
A DIVISION OF HAY HOUSE

Balboa Press books may be ordered through booksellers or by contacting:

Balboa Press
A Division of Hay House
1663 Liberty Drive
Bloomington, IN 47403
www.balboapress.com
1 (877) 407-4847

Because of the dynamic nature of the Internet, any web addresses or links contained in this book may have changed since publication and may no longer be valid. The views expressed in this work are solely those of the author and do not necessarily reflect the views of the publisher, and the publisher hereby disclaims any responsibility for them.

The author of this book does not dispense medical advice or prescribe the use of any technique as a form of treatment for physical, emotional, or medical problems without the advice of a physician, either directly or indirectly. The intent of the author is only to offer information of a general nature to help you in your quest for emotional and spiritual well-being. In the event you use any of the information in this book for yourself, which is your constitutional right, the author and the publisher assume no responsibility for your actions.

Any people depicted in stock imagery provided by Thinkstock are models, and such images are being used for illustrative purposes only.
Certain stock imagery © Thinkstock.

Printed in the United States of America.

ISBN: 978-1-4525-9761-4 (sc)
ISBN: 978-1-4525-9762-1 (hc)
ISBN: 978-1-4525-9779-9 (e)

Library of Congress Control Number: 2014919081

Balboa Press rev. date: 11/26/2014

Contents

Illustration

Tables

For
Marilyn J. Hochman
and her family

The eternal quest of the individual human being is to shatter his loneliness.

--Norman Cousins

Forward

In 2012 I attended a SENG (Supporting the Emotional Needs of the Gifted) Conference in Milwaukee, Wisconsin. I was just beginning my journey toward grasping the meaning of "giftedness." Whereas I once believed gifted solely represented higher intelligence or intellect, SENG allowed me a holistic understanding of the strengths and challenges of gifted, including: intensities, sensitivities, excitabilities, emotionality and asynchronies. Through this understanding I am currently able to successfully strategize and advocate for gifted parents and children.

At that Milwaukee conference I attended my very first session, "Six Steps Toward Joyful Living" given by Dianne Allen. It was standing room only and I had no idea how my life, and that of my family, was about to change forever. Dianne led us through self-revelations, spiritual, energetic, and physically inspiring exercises, and gave us advice, connection and clarity. Every person left that room on an elevated plane.

Part of understanding and teaching joyful living however, requires Dianne to fully understand one of the enemies of joy – loneliness. Through Dianne's experience as a counselor and coach to gifted clients suffering from addiction, and from her vantage point as a highly gifted and self-proclaimed "introvert," Dianne affords the reader an understanding of loneliness from an authentic place.

Dianne takes her raw experience and information and establishes a strategy – a model– for transformation. As with Dianne's approach to living joyfully, the first step in curing loneliness is through daily consistent focused action. Not only does <u>The Loneliness Cure</u> provide the reader a visual Model for Transformation, but peppers its pages with exercises and even a chart to help the reader realize where (s)he can help her/himself. Whereas Dianne teaches that connection is vital for joyful living, so too disconnection fuels loneliness. Dianne realizes that loneliness, like joyfulness, affects all people.

So how do we go from loneliness and negatively affecting those around us to joyfulness and transmitting that positive energy? Dianne argues for strategic connections, purposeful pathways that connect us to logical partners and friends. It is in making these thoughtful, meaningful connections that we remain connected to our own true essence and can combat loneliness. Awareness, however, of our true essence and purpose is necessary for authentic and deep connections within oneself and to others.

I am privileged to say that Dianne Allen continues as a mentor but is now also my friend. She has taught me that joyfulness indicates an internal equilibrium, knowing who you are and feeling good about it. This representation of joyfulness is the cure to loneliness. Dianne's spiritual giftedness allows her to communicate and connect with people on a deeper level and to truly show people how to become their own personal agents of change.

Julie F. Skolnick, Esq., M.A., J.D.
With Understanding Comes Calm, LLC
Supporting Parents of Gifted and Distractible Children
withunderstandingcomescalm.com
Potomac, MD
August, 2014

Preface

Loneliness and the fear of being lonely are blamed for many of the poor decisions and poor behavior in all walks of life. Recently I facilitated a workshop and when asked about their most powerful fear, nearly 80% of all participants mentioned loneliness or being afraid to be alone in their responses. For me, this was remarkable. The high majority of the group was afraid of loneliness. This audience was composed of smart, successful, animated people who were admittedly secretly struggling with loneliness and the fear of this experience. Naturally, I began to throw the question out more frequently in my work as well as my social life. I began to examine the underlying aspects within me. What I found was an almost universal undercurrent of fear in people and for many it included the fear of being alone in life which was translated into fear of loneliness. With this information and the prevalence in the people I was working with as well as others, I began to seek options for people to heal loneliness as well as release the fear of being alone.

The fear of being alone seems to transcend age and gender. The consequent poor behaviors appear to range from minor to life altering. One woman disclosed remaining in an abusive relationship with her boyfriend because she was afraid to be alone. A young man shared his overeating and video game addiction to avoid feeling lonely. An executive shared how he would work long hours and add to his stress in order to not be alone, even with his family wanting to have him available. He simply was not yet able to allow his relationships to support him. Everyone was cheated. The stories went on and on.

Loneliness, the feeling or experience of being alone or separate from your source is a spiritual issue. The disconnection is in the area of life that is our connection to the greater world. I notice that many people make choices regarding loneliness as if it is a physical issue. Feeling lonely often yields interesting results; actively seeking a person or animal to fill the ever present void in their physical lives. These situations are often short lasting or become toxic because the identified solution does not correlate to the real challenge. Attempting to fix spiritual issues with a physical action alone will not yield lasting and powerful results.

Imagine for a minute that you are fully aligned with who you are and where you are going in life. I'll bet that your actions and words would be very different than the behaviors you do when fearful of being alone. How often have you compromised yourself because you were afraid of being alone?

The issue is you being disconnected from you. It cannot be solved by distracting with another person or action. No matter the predicament you find yourself, there are steps that can reconnect you with you. When you are connected within and acting on your connection, loneliness is impossible. Remember connection within is the correction.

The powerful and inspiring result of freeing yourself from loneliness is contentment. Contentment is a combination of happiness, satisfaction, fulfillment and gratitude. Many people wonder if these feelings are possible. They are possible and this book will show you the way to transformation from loneliness to contentment.

Acknowledgements

I would first like to acknowledge the creative energy that is moving in and through all of us. The ideas and concepts in this book have been begging to be shared. Many nights I have awakened with these ideas coming forth. I am grateful.

I acknowledge Julie F. Skolnick for her willingness to write the forward for this book. She has inspired me in rich and authentic ways. Thank you also to Crystal Gifford for reading and reviewing the manuscript. Thank you to Maryellen Patterson for her consistent support throughout the entire process.

I am grateful to my many friends, colleagues and guides who have all had a significant impact on me and this book. I want to thank Carol Miele for reviewing this manuscript and offering wonderful suggestions and ideas. Thanks also to JoJo Davoli for encouraging and believing in my work on a daily basis. Many thanks go to Lisa Marshall for her consistent encouragement and support over many years.

Thank you to all the countless people who have helped me write this book. Many of the influential people are not even aware of their significant role in this text. There are the visionaries and thinkers who have gone before me, most of whom I will never know personally, yet whose work has made my work possible.

I offer humble gratitude to SENG (Supporting Emotional Needs of Gifted), Dr. James Webb, Dr. Susan Daniels and others who have pioneered and continue to further the work with bright and talented youth and adults.

I want to acknowledge Maggie Mae. She is the most amazing loving and angelic labradoodle. Every part of her being loves and supports me and my work. Her unconditional love transcends words.

Finally, this book would not be possible without the unwavering support of my spiritual family and close contacts. I am truly humbled by your presence and passion for this work.

Introduction – Are you lonely?

"He that is discontented in one place will seldom
be happy in another." ~ Aesop

Ever since I can remember, I have been lonely. I was a quiet,
introverted and smart young child. I built my identity by immersing
myself into the lives of others around me; I had no life of my own.
In high school, I remember being at an event for the Senior Board. I
was looking at my peers playing pool and socializing. Sitting on the
couch I remember thinking "I am an alien, this makes no sense to
me and I don't really belong." I spent most of the night wondering
in silence why I was even there and if anyone even noticed me. I
remember touching my face because the pain of the separation
was so powerful that I wondered if my face had somehow become
plastic. Was I depressed or just shy or introverted? I didn't know
what it was.

I never related to many people my age. In fact, my teenage
birthday parties were attended equally by adults from my sailing
world and my teenage friends. My parents partied with the teenagers
so this was natural. I remember a party where there was one room
of adults and another of my peers. I was so confused yet I was
special somehow to be having such an experience. I related better
to the adults.

Today, nearly 5 decades later, I look around and see that
loneliness is a pervasive problem in our society. Was it always

this big of a problem or has the industrial age and electronics created a new host of challenges for humans? I recently asked the ones around me about loneliness and every person reported they could relate. Several said that they often feel lonely when there are plenty of people around. This reminded me of a seminar that I presented where a large number of both men and women reported being afraid to be alone. The fear of loneliness was keeping them in unhealthy situations, they knew it yet they kept on; ever afraid of being alone. So, here I sat, with people choosing unhappiness and in some cases violence over the potential of being alone. This was extraordinary for me to hear the way these people shared. They concluded that the fear of being alone was so powerful that they would remain in toxic, abusive situations in order to "have someone". One person said "someone is better than no one and I don't want to be lonely anymore." Wow, this was startling to me even though I myself have felt similarly and I have worked with many clients over the past years that have parallel stories.

In my work as a counselor and mentor, I encounter loneliness in many ways and with many labels attached. Any form of addiction creates a sense of isolation and loneliness which is a cornerstone of the disease process in addiction. Engaging in what could be called unacceptable behavior leaves the person suffering from a sense of isolation and loneliness that is perpetuated by the belief that "no one would understand or believe me." Often these people had been experiencing some type of loneliness for many years, partly addiction related and partly socially related. Nonetheless, loneliness was an obvious component in their struggles. I have worked with people who had an ex-boyfriend or ex-girlfriend commit suicide over a break up. The fear of being alone or being alone was so unbearable these people took their life. Now, the others also have survivor's guilt. The overarching problem has ripple effects that impact all people.

Some of my recent work has been around the topic of Joy and Passion in living. When I reflect on my personal history, this appears curious to me initially as to how these topics are so prevalent in my work. Could it be that having lived in and somehow transcended the loneliness paradigm, I can see the issue more clearly? Today, I know that loneliness and being alone are totally different things. The source of each is different even though they may be related at times in the human experience. Loneliness is a spiritual disconnection while being alone is a physical situation. Seeking another person will not ease loneliness at its root. You may be distracted for a bit. Many folks report continuing to feel lonely even when they are with another or a group. So, people alone cannot and do not fix or solve loneliness.

I have been asking myself about this issue on many levels over some time. Many people seem to experience some level of loneliness in their lifetime. Most people begin to see that regaining connection is a large part of the correction for their life trajectory. Being lonely over an extended period of time can cause depression, anger outbursts, resentments, blaming language, tearfulness, and addictions of all kinds, poor relationships, and poor decision making overall and low self-esteem. Other issues and challenges are also associated with loneliness or the perception of loneliness.

Humans are meant to be in relation with one another. Thus loneliness is a disruption in the growth and thriving ability of a person who experiences loneliness. Trying to convince this person that: "See, there are people around you" doesn't help much if the person cannot connect or feel the others around them. It is the connection to others _and_ one self _and_ one's higher self that dissipates loneliness. Decreasing the angst and pain of loneliness in life is an important part of regaining joy, freedom and success.

This book will discuss the many causes of loneliness, the many faces of loneliness, the consequences of loneliness and how to rid you of loneliness. Introverted or extroverted, loneliness hinders your happiness and stunts your growth. It is a formidable foe due to the insidious nature of the impact in our lives from the personal to the national and global. I hope to offer viable ideas, suggestions and solutions that you may use to ease your angst or the angst of a loved one. Illustrations and stories and anecdotes will be used to help illustrate ideas. I trust they will be helpful for you.

Though the stories are fictional, you may find aspects of yourself within the characters. This is because some of the human condition is universal. Often loneliness can create the belief that you are alone in your pain and disconnection. This is an error. All people, from time to time, deal with loneliness. It robs you of happiness, joy and authentic connection with yourself and others. It is a good idea to have a journal handy while reading this book. Document your personal ideas, challenges and solutions. It is not possible to cover every facet of this topic in one text. Your thoughts and ideas are unique to you and should be written for your future reference.

It is my hope that you will spend time with this book and the suggestions. Keep track of your ideas and actions. You will be able to see the power of synergy and focus as you take action and note the results. Remain open minded and allow the words to speak to your heart. From my heart to yours, may you experience the freedom and contentment you deserve.

PART I

Loneliness

Chapter 1

Impact of Loneliness

In this chapter, I will discuss the impact of loneliness in personal life, family life, social life, cultural life, and global life. The depths of loneliness can be so dark that it may seem that life is no longer worth it. Many people have also experienced varied depths of darkness. Loneliness is part of the human condition that reflects our disconnection from our Source. Humans tend to want to be connected. This is because we are wired for connection in order to thrive.

Personal

Personal loneliness is a phenomenon that is evident all around. It is that deep inner sense of being disconnected from oneself, other people or from the source of life itself. You might be thinking of times that you have experienced significant loneliness as you read these pages. You might even be experiencing deep loneliness right now. Personal loneliness is that loneliness that reminds you that on a deep, often existential level you are alone in this world yet there is the ability and or opportunity to be connected which seems like a paradox. No matter the apparent cause, loneliness impacts people in many significant ways. You may tend to withdraw from people or you might even decline invitations or become "hermit like". The impact of loneliness in your personal life includes social separation, depression, frustration, anger, physical stress and disease of the body, as well as an overall sense of hopelessness in daily life. Clearly, these impacts are simply a few of the major issues that you might be experiencing in times when loneliness grips your life experience.

Most people experience these difficulties from time to time and some people do not even try to change it because they don't believe that it is possible. Thus personal loneliness seems to be part of the human condition that most people tend to live with rather than transform and evolve through. You may even use distractions to avoid the issue all together.

Familial

You might be experiencing a level of loneliness and this personal loneliness also is part of family loneliness which can impact the functioning of any family system. These family systems include your biological immediate family your family of choice and/or your spiritual family. When you are brought together in a family type relationship setting, you can see that personal loneliness affects the family. Some families become lonely and separated due to external circumstances like judgment, perceived upset or somehow having broken societal rules. Some families experience loneliness and separation because of the actions of a family member within the family that then impacts the family's place within the community. Some families experience family loneliness because of a cultural norm or religious judgment that sets them apart from and thus isolates them from the culture at large.

Families, who are isolated, tend also to be what I call a closed system. Imagine the Dead Sea, with an inlet but no outlet. The salt content becomes so high that nothing can live in its waters. This similar phenomenon can happen in some families. What happens is that there is information coming from the outside. The information stays within the closed system and never is allowed to evolve or emerge through the family back out into the world. Thus this flow of energy and the flow of understanding stop. Members of the family become increasingly isolated, agitated, resentful or depressed. This closed system does not serve the family members within the system and it does not serve the greater good of any other families around them. This situation appears to be ever-increasing. You might experience the kind of family loneliness from a family that has the rule "tell the truth except when it's about this family." The implication here is that you can be free and open and honest as long as you do not allow anything about the family to get out. For members of this family this level of fear of reprisal, creates personal and then family loneliness. It is clear that many of the ongoing old cultural beliefs must be reevaluated and transformed for their usefulness as we move forward in this culture.

Societal

Societal loneliness can be very pervasive and also hidden. It is in the judgment of others based on who their group might be. The up-and-coming people from one particular area may judge people from another area as if they are stupid or otherwise less than. There are people in one group judging another group because they don't understand certain food choices or behaviors. There are many examples of greater societal judgment within our own country here in the United States. You can also see this level of judgment that is within societies from this country toward another country or any other countries. Indigenous or native folks tend to be judged by others without any investigation as to validity or understanding of customs or ideas. To protect themselves, the societies must turn inward and create a form of barrier between them and others. Initially this barrier which could include an actual wall or simply just no communication is meant to be protective. In the beginning it is protective. If the barrier is left unchecked or allowed to continue to grow, this group then becomes lonely which increases isolation and then once again everything becomes stagnant. Loneliness in the entire group of people within the society becomes a pervasive challenge.

Society and isolation within a society also can be from one paradigm to another paradigm. People who see things from a spiritual or religious avenue may differ completely from somebody who sees things more secularly. You would notice this also in a situation if you were the only republican working in a predominately democratic office or the other way around where your views might appear different than those around. It seems that people will often accept this level of disconnection that causes pain and discord as just part of life. Living in and passively accepting loneliness and disconnection hinders your growth and transformation. People are meant to be connected, meant to be honored and meant to experience being a part of the greater humanity.

Some societies have segments that have been or are oppressed. Regardless of the reason for the oppression, when the oppression is lifted and the members of the oppressed group are liberated, there is rejoicing initially. All too often, those same recently freed can become angry and violent. On the surface the anger seems unwarranted. Bystanders may question and judge the people as ungrateful. Consider being oppressed for your lifetime or even generations and then things change and you are no longer held back and you can see beyond the wall that you had been behind all those years. After the celebration, deep pain and anguish begins to surface. The energy of the deep, unspeakable pain explodes forth in anger. There is a deep and pervasive human condition that acts this cycle out every day. It is noble to want to free a society or group within a society. It is compassionate to also be present to heal the grief and pain. Freeing a group and leaving them to figure it out from there can backfire and end up being a disservice rather than a service. It is time to really examine the larger picture then act from the larger view for the healing and subsequent freedom and joy for all.

Cultural

Cultural loneliness has been seen most profoundly within different religious cultures. I know people from many different cultures who have different spiritual or religious viewpoints. You may be able to identify different cultures from yourself and notice how they become isolated and therefore experience a sense of loneliness based on where they are or what they might believe. A simple language difference and ability to communicate or not communicate within the larger culture can create a sense of loneliness and isolation. The United States after all is a melting pot. Initially many cultures with many languages trying to come together yet isolated are set up for the potential of loneliness from the very beginning. If you are the only Spanish-speaking person in an entire city who are speaking Greek, then not only are you isolated personally or maybe with your family, you are culturally isolated from your Greek neighbors. They may not truly understand your ways, how you celebrate holidays how you honor certain things down to even the food that you cook. What if you were placed in a situation where the food that you consider normal, the food that you enjoy, is unavailable due to the culture in which you live? If you are part of the majority within the culture, this may seem a little foreign to you. I invite you to look around you and see your world in a way that will help you identify how cultural loneliness creates further disconnection and a sense of isolation and holds all of humanity back due to the separation.

Global

You might be wondering what global loneliness could possibly be. If the common experience of humans, the human condition if you will, includes that of loneliness which is a sense of separation or disconnection, then global loneliness is a current epidemic. After all, fear is reflection of a sense of separation and lack of trust and safety in the world at large. When you become upset or fearful you are separated from your source. You are lonely when anyone creates a separation or experiences loneliness and the entire globe is affected.

Think about those people, those societies, those others that are different than you. Do you welcome them into your life fully and completely without judgment as part of the greater human family? I'd venture that most of us would have a caveat or condition under which we would say yes to that question. Any hesitation caveat or condition warranted or not, would signal for you that loneliness and/or fear is part of the cultural and global world epidemic.

As with your family and community, you must learn good boundaries and proper discernment. Global loneliness is not a suggestion to accept unacceptable behavior in the name of healing loneliness. Global and personal respect and safety are part of the healing of loneliness. Remember that connection, authentic connection, is the correction. In the event that connection is not the motivator of some individuals, then true transcendence of loneliness will be slower to manifest. When a person or groups of people are fearful for any reason, disconnection from source and others can yield more painful and hurtful actions.

It is sound judgment to not continue to enter the lion's den expecting the lion to somehow magically have changed into a house cat. You as a free thinking and able human being are called to use good discernment in your choice of actions. Naively putting yourself in harm's way may not serve the highest good. Again, use good discernment for what is right for you to do.

When you take the time to look at your own life circumstance, you may notice that loneliness is a piece of every time you have struggled in your life. Loneliness can cause you to take actions that do not serve you. Loneliness can create a sleepless night that leads to crying or upset that leads to agitation frustration or resentment that then can lead to depression or an anger outburst. Loneliness can be seen as the seed that lodged within your being that can create havoc in many areas of your life. Because your personal life affects your family and your society and your culture and our globe, it is critical that each one begin to heal and close up the wound of loneliness that is within all humans. You must remember that every time you heal a wound of loneliness within yourself, you will in fact heal all of those associated with you on every level past, present, and future.

This book is largely coming to you from my professional and human experience. The devastating impact of loneliness for people suffering from many forms of hidden pain and isolation or old grief and fears is prevalent. The traumatic signs of loneliness can be seen in successful working professionals who have no viable peer group, and who have created a sense of isolation in order to "make it" in the world. The amazing power of loneliness is evident when people shrink and hide and deny their own value for fear that they might be seen in an authentic manner. Loneliness, I believe is part of every one of our lives directly and indirectly. The impact is staggering. Every time I go online, watch the news, or read the paper, I see the acting out of people feeling lonely. Now they may not call it loneliness because somehow in this culture that word is associated often with people who are weak or somehow unable. This simply is not the case. Many successful people struggle with a deep sense of loneliness which is the cause of their frenetic action that has created their success. This is one way that success becomes toxic success and can bring down very talented successful individuals. The paradox is that the extra work and the stress of having to fight off loneliness to be successful cause them to pay a very large price. Often these people end up with dysfunctional situations in their relationships multiple medical issues whether they address them or not from heart disease to diabetes to joint pain and all kinds of other problems. In order to be "successful" as the society dictates, and to run from the loneliness and the fear of loneliness, these type people work excessively. This working to the bone literally is an out picturing of what loneliness often looks like. These people might even receive accolades or rewards for all of their work. What they need to know is that there is a better way; they will be able to achieve more by shifting their paradigm.

Harry's Story

In Harry's story you will be able to identify aspects and consequences of loneliness within your own life. Harry is a successful married business executive with 2 loving adult children. His wife of over 25 years loves and is devoted to her husband and children. Harry's children, ages 23 and 21 are living in different cities and Harry sees them several times a year and he speaks to them frequently. Harry speaks about being lonely even with his loving family and it is starting to negatively affect his marriage. Arguments are erupting where they never would have previously. Harry is recently retired and he is now home more than ever before. Harry shares that he worked very hard during his career which has afforded his wife and children many good things over the years. He said "It used to be all about the money. If I made a lot of money then everyone would be happy forever." Harry shares how he would work hard, take promotions that would relocate the family even when the family objected. He truly believed that making money would take care of everything and everyone.

In retirement, as Harry tells the story sitting on his back deck overlooking the expanse of the beach and the water, he has tears in his eyes. "If only I could see where this was heading, I would have made different choices" said Harry. Harry took a long slow deep breath, gazed out over the water and then exhaled. The silence was palpable and Harry's pain and loneliness was evident, without a word spoken. Did he ruin his life and his family's lives? How could it have gotten to this point? What is his purpose anyway if making money didn't work and he is not making any now anyway? Was it all a sham? Harry is struggling with his deep feeling of loneliness that he was able to fend off his entire adult life until now. What went wrong?

We sat and shared about the good times and his wonderful adventures with his family and his successful career. Harry offered a lot to others in his career, he knew that. In his travels and his many adventures, he reflected on often feeling alone in the wee hours of the morning when everyone else was asleep. Harry would wake up and feel the pressures and feel alone and then decide to not say anything and keep pressing on toward the financial goals. Now that the goals have been attained and he is retired earlier than his peers, Harry sits alone, quietly sad and grieving. This is not how he imagined things turning out for him. How come everyone else around seemed happy and he is so quietly alone on the inside.

Harry shared that his wife is noticing that something is not right yet Harry says nothing. This is what the arguing is over. Harry's wife thinks he is hiding something and Harry feels miserable yet cannot identify the source so he denies the feeling to protect her feelings. This has become convoluted all in the name of love and with little awareness of the power of loneliness and internal isolation.

Harry questions his value and purpose in retirement while his wife is excited to have her husband home. Harry shared his long term feeling of being alone. He said it has been in his hidden life since childhood and has nothing to do with his family. If anything, their love and devotion has helped him and yet now, without the work distraction, Harry is alone and isolated once again in his inner world.

With some conversation and guidance and support, Harry began to see how loneliness and not being truly connected to his source and higher self has led to this spot in life. Harry, having a PhD in Literature, was not interested in dogma. Using the concepts of energy and like seeking like, Harry could see how his running from feeling alone actually kept perpetuating itself within his creative distractions over his lifetime.

Harry and I worked toward developing an inner connection and sense of inherent value. Harry began to change. His face relaxed and his wife shared that he started laughing again. Harry now began every morning with some quiet, meditation time. Sometimes he would take a long walk on the beach; other times sit quietly and reflect. Harry began to transform a life of hidden angst into a life of peace and fulfillment. As his sense of being *alone* internally waned, his relationships with himself and others transformed. As the new way of living began to work, Harry could see the long term stress and grief that feeling alone and isolated over many years has caused.

Checking back with Harry several months after the completion of our work together, he reported having lost weight, improved his diet, traveled and visited his mother and his children and a deeper sense of intimacy with his wife. Harry shared his gratitude for being shown that when he lives from the inside out rather than externally motivated, he is happier and healthier. Harry said: "I am no longer lonely or even afraid of being alone because I am connected to my purpose and value. All the other benefits are icing on the cake. Thank you."

As long as Harry continues to nurture his inner life and connection, he will thrive. Harry was able to learn and use a new way to live. Harry is just one example of a person who was able to connect within and create joy and passion beyond what he ever thought was possible.

Conclusion

By reading this book and learning the techniques shared in it, you will be better able to heal the wounds and the limiting beliefs that hold you in a prison of loneliness. It would be irrational to expect that reading a book will fix the problem. It would be rational to believe that taking daily consistent focused action will in fact yield for you; a life beyond your wildest dreams. The key here and the solution to loneliness lie in creating connection in multiple areas of your life. In the next chapter, we will begin to look at some of the major causes of loneliness. This will help you personally identify and apply the ideas, concepts and actions that are suggested in this book.

This book is not meant to be a comprehensive guide for everything and everyone at all times. It is meant to be a practical way to help you awaken and create beautiful ideas for your own health and your own happiness. You may identify causes for your own loneliness that I do not address. It is a good idea to note those ideas in a journal or on some paper that you can refer to as the book unfolds. Do not rely on your memory to remember the ideas you have at a later time because memory changes over time and you may or may not be able to recall what you're thinking about as you read. Have a pen and paper and write your ideas as you read so that you will be able to gain all that you can from reading this text.

Chapter 2

Causes of Loneliness

The causes of loneliness are endless. It seems that some sort of loneliness on one or more levels is what plagues each person who begins to seek a better way of living. Here I would like to discuss some of the major causes of loneliness and how they interface or feed into other areas of challenges in our lives.

Fear

Fear is likely the most pervasive, prevalent, and powerful cause of loneliness for each person who experiences that sense of separation. Fear of the future, fear of success, fear of failure and the list goes on. The function of the feeling of fear is to "get ready". The way most people experience the feeling of being fearful could fall into three major categories: flight, fight and freeze.

The first category is flight. Flight can be physically leaving a space or mentally checking out and thinking of something else including emotionally shutting down or going within. Flight is very common and it is not always the physical leaving of the situation that will let you know the person is experiencing flight. You may have experienced flight from yourself or another when in a conversation the topic becomes emotionally difficult and suddenly it is difficult to pay attention or you or the other person day dreams and needs to be reminded to come back to the conversation.

The second category is fight. People can fight physically, verbally and mentally. Fighting is not just physical altercation. Fighting can be an argument or a debate or a passive aggressive kind of behavior aimed at drawing another person in to discord. Fighting is highly reinforced in our culture particularly with men.

The third category is freeze. Freezing is when the fear level becomes so high that the person is unable, due to being overwhelmed, to function to complete daily tasks. A person who has frozen often does not think very clearly, or act in a way that is productive or helpful. Freeze is very common for people suffering from some form of an anxiety or addiction. When the addiction or anxiety becomes overwhelming or has progressed to a certain point, often that person is unable to come out of this frozen space in order to take an action for their own best interest. Fear causes tremendous, exquisite loneliness in our society.

Loneliness and fear appear to be related somehow. There are times when loneliness initiates the fear. I have seen times where fear and the actions one takes while afraid create loneliness. Regardless of the order or intensity, fear and loneliness tend to go hand in hand. You might want to look at your life and see where fear and loneliness intersect or feed off of each other. Now this is a time to be very honest internally, most people do not want to admit to feeling lonely or to being afraid.

The fear I am talking about is not simply being emotionally afraid of something like a spider or a bug. The fear I am talking about is the energy, the feeling that keeps us separated from the safety and beauty of this world and your life. Sometimes the fear shows up in ways that there are no words to describe yet you may experience a hesitation or inner resistance to following your heart's desires in a healthy manner. This existential fear is often at the root of excuses for not taking healthy actions. What would happen if your heart's desire really did come to pass? How would your life change if you released fear and loneliness and accepted the assistance and love that is all around?

Pain

Pain causes loneliness and loneliness causes pain. Again these two go together in perfect ways. Have you ever experienced a time when someone you cared about was in pain of some kind? Maybe the person was depressed or sad. Maybe the person had physical diagnosis that was causing them pain. How easy was it for you to go and be with that person, sitting with them in their experience without judgment or running? The pain in this situation can cause loneliness for the person experiencing it because many people don't know what to do or say when someone they care for is struggling or seriously ill. In the Western society there is a great deal of avoidance and people saying "I don't know what to do", so they do nothing. That is fear and pain coming together to keep both people isolated and lonely. Both the person who has the pain who is yearning for connection as well as the person who wants to connect are unable or simply do not know how to connect to relieve pain and loneliness. So here, loneliness and pain and fear come together in a way that creates even more challenges and separation.

You might want to look at areas in your life where pain is prevalent. Ask yourself if these pain areas in any way impact a sense of isolation or loneliness for yourself or others. Pain areas of your life could include: being promoted at work from one of the guys to a boss, having a medical diagnosis that confounds your friends or family, experiencing a physical injury that now limits you from previous actions or activities, a relationship breakdown that causes a change of associations, or making a decision to change an area of your life and therefore having to change who you associate with and what you do with your time. The experience of pain as part of the loneliness cycle has many facets and is often difficult to even put into words. When you experience any major shift in your behavior or attitude or way of being then there is a sense of pain or grief as the old must leave and the new enters. So even getting married or having a baby or another exciting life event can also create a level of pain and loneliness due to the change and separation from what was historically the situation.

Walter and Sophie's Story

Walter and Sophie were very much in love. They had been engaged for over two years and soon they would be married. Happy and excited, both focused on a successful life ahead. Both Walter and Sophie had been devoted to each other. The wedding was everything they imagined. All their friends and family were present to witness the great occasion. Their parents seemed anxious at times yet they declined to talk about their apparent anxiety.

Walter and Sophie went on a honeymoon that fulfilled a long time dream to travel throughout Europe. Overseas, just the two of them for two full weeks. No interference from family or friends. Walter focused on the adventure of going away while Sophie was focused on quiet time alone.

Shortly after they came home, Sophie called. She was crying, she reported that Walter was aloof and distant – not the same. A few days later, Walter called and was expressing his upset about the beginning of the marriage being fraught with arguments and distance between them.

Independently of each other, both Sophie and Walter contacted me for advice on what to do because of the arguing and discord; neither had prepared for the grief and letting go of the previous life. Their ways as individuals had changed to being a couple and they had not accounted for the changes. Becoming a couple, a desired change, still requires each person to let go of history and the way things used to be in order to embrace the new way of moving through the world. I encouraged each to share their feelings with each other. I also supported taking time to let go of the past with honor and respect. Only then, could they move forward into the marriage they imagined.

As time unfolded, both Walter and Sophie released their fantasies about the past and their attempt to hold on to the single life while being married and having a partner in life. They created new family traditions and new rhythms for their marriage that supported their relationship. There were adjustments to be made with regard to friends, family and work activities yet both of them now were focused on the good of their union and each other rather than acting out of fear and pain of what they lost.

Anger

Anger can be another cause of loneliness. Angry resentful upset people can create loneliness for themselves in ways like no other. Even someone who is silently angry can push others away and create loneliness for themselves that is intense and often cutting to the heart. Some people have anger in their demeanor and way of being that is so familiar to them that they are not able to identify the agitation as a form of anger. Any place in your life where rapport breaks down or some form of disconnection happens; anger may be one of the conscious or unconscious causes of the loneliness that ensues.

There are many words that indicate anger on some level. Not all anger looks the same or feels the same. Intolerance, frustration, pity and discord are all various levels and types of anger. Depression is anger turned inward and can cause self-harm just like aggression causes harm to others.

I have heard it said that when violence becomes part of the society's entertainment that a downward spiral of disintegration is happening. If that is true, then our society is in trouble. I believe that the anger and loneliness synergy is what literally blows up things. People are so frustrated to the point of road rage and yelling at others for no viable reason. Resentments create distance and no communication within families that then sustains great loneliness. You may have also many different examples of how anger large or small creates loneliness: for the person feeling anger as well as the person experiencing it coming from another. Our societal acceptance of anger in its many forms is perpetuating loneliness that perpetuates the search to feel less lonely that keeps a cycle of generational distance and pain alive. It is time to make changes so that loneliness will no longer be such a prevalent human condition that it is everywhere.

Addictions

Addiction is widespread throughout the globe and affects every person alive. Addiction is continuing a behavior that you know is hurting you but you cannot stop. Addiction is predictably unpredictable. This means that the person outside of you can predict that you cannot predict what you will do once you engage in the behavior. Addiction is not just to alcohol or drugs. Addiction is applicable to loneliness, gambling, sex, anger, fear, food, violence, relationships, control and the list goes on. If you were to anthropomorphize addiction in its raw way, you would see that it preys on creating and then maintaining a sense of loneliness for the victim. The person who is addicted is lonely to the depth that not even they can explain most of the time. Addictive behaviors and substances work best in the darkness thereby creating an intense and pervasive sense of isolation and loneliness. The loneliness and despair in addiction and early recovery is often very intense that some are not sure how to manage life and continue to survive. These people were not suicidal. These people were attempting to simply describe the intensity of the darkness of what addiction does to one's sense of connection. Remembering that loneliness is a sign of disconnection we can see that as addiction progresses and disconnection continues that loneliness gets more and more intense.

Now, when your arm falls asleep and goes numb and you move it to get the blood back in it, it hurts more before it feels better. That tingly intense feeling of the blood finally getting back into your arm hurts for a moment prior to feeling better, right? This is the same for someone who has addiction in their life. When a person chooses another way, often the loneliness may feel more intense before true connections begin to heal the previous loneliness. Be encouraged to remember this so that in your own healing process or the healing process of someone you love this will not be forgotten. Often life can seem worse before it gets better. In the beginning this might mean that you are on the right track. This is why support systems and people who understand are very important when trying to make major life changes. It is best to have your support system consist of people who are independent of your family or anyone else who is emotionally involved with your success or not. The closer someone is to you, the more difficult objectivity and real solutions can appear.

Addictions in all its forms cause loneliness. When you are isolated from others and from your own inner wisdom due to an addiction, you are vulnerable to further isolation, secrecy and loneliness. The cycle perpetuates until there is a crisis or disruption of some kind that can shine the light on viable solutions for your loneliness. Most addictions are insidious and can hide behind pride, self-righteousness, willpower and spirituality. Still, the impact remains and you bring to the experience more and more loneliness as the cycle progresses. Make the decision to be honest and accept feedback and input from trusted others. Try on the feedback and see where it leads. Be open and remember that all people have a blind spot. Input from trusted others is helpful on all levels. Journaling your ideas and experiences helps keep you on track.

Spiritual Bankruptcy

Spiritual bankruptcy is a phrase that refers to someone who denies or is disconnected from their spiritual essence. This has nothing to do with religion or religious practices. This has everything to do with you being connected to who you are, why you are here on Earth, and what is your personal mission. Your spiritual essence speaks to your purpose and mission on this earth. It is much larger than what you do for a living or where you live or who you associate with daily. When you become spiritually bankrupt you are so distant from your own sense of who you are and what you're doing, that you often become apathetic, depressed, and increasingly isolated which feeds the loneliness. To begin the work many report that they have lost connection with who they are and what they're doing with their life. Some people will report a lot of pain, because they know what they should be doing and can't seem to do it. Others might not have any idea at all, thereby feeling lonely because they are not aware of what is theirs to do. If your situation is either of these two examples or another, spiritual bankruptcy will wreak havoc in your life and create loneliness until you finally, finally come to yourself and say yes to who you truly are and what you're truly meant to do.

Don's Story

Don is a smart man. He is well educated, being both a teacher and an attorney. Don's career brought him to a location over a thousand miles from his family and hometown. Don is an introvert and enjoys contemplation and reading. He didn't think that moving away would create any challenges. Don did not account for his emotional and spiritual needs when making his plans. Don reports being disconnected from his family because of life choices and geographic distance.

Don thrived initially with his new life and career. He learned the job well and he liked the new environment. The warmer weather was a welcome change. After several months, Don began to experience a sense of loneliness and sadness. He called his family less. He woke up on Sunday morning and realized he had no friends in his new location. He had work acquaintances yet had not begun any new friendships. Don had a sinking feeling in his stomach. He spent the day, thinking and contemplating his life. Don took no action except to contemplate. This began the cycle that ended him in spiritual bankruptcy, feeling lonely and disconnected.

By the end of the day, Don realized that he had no idea what he was doing with his life any longer. He couldn't even say he was happy or not happy. He was just flat, surviving without a sense of purpose. Don used his linear, problem solving ability that has been highly rewarded in his career to attempt to figure out what went wrong and how. All day, he thought and figured to no avail.

Don contacted me at the suggestion of a friend. He was somewhat resistant but he said he would talk with me to get his friend off his back. After some discussion, I suggested to Don that an aspect of his loneliness and seeming "depression" was being separated from his personal mission. Don had become ever so slowly disconnected from what fueled his soul and kept the twinkle in his eye. He was dying a slow spiritual death. I shared with Don the idea of spiritual bankruptcy. I explained the nature of no sense of self or connection to the greater even though he was working and producing by the society's standards. His inner life and sense of value had slowly drained away while he was looking outside of himself for validation.

Don began to see the impact of this deep isolation and loneliness that can be hidden within what appears to be a successful career. Over time, Don began to make changes in his daily routine and his focus on his personal heart's desires. Don slowly began to get the bounce in his step and the brightness in his eyes started to return. Don laughed spontaneously once again and he was back on track. Spiritual bankruptcy can impact anyone. It is a reflection of being somehow out of touch with connection to the greater purpose of life. Being connected within allows for better connections without.

Now, many months later, Don recounts his journey as one into and then out of darkness. Don spends time each day connecting within and then taking action in alignment with his personal mission; all of this within the context of his daily professional and family life. Don shared that his initial resistance was a fear and now he is glad he understands the power of spiritual connection. Don shares with others the importance of daily spiritual deposits to "keep your balance in the black". Don is no longer spiritually bankrupt.

Intergenerational Transmission of Pain

Intergenerational transmission of pain is a profound and deep source of loneliness in our world today. Many of the painful and difficult lessons of our ancestors are being passed down generation to generation without understanding of the huge consequences. You might be dealing with loneliness and isolation and pain and grief that was started and then perpetuated many generations before you. If your mother was raised in a family where her mother told her and her mother's mother told her that to be a woman meant you could not have a career, and you a young girl wanted a career, you either shrink and not follow your career choice which is loneliness or you comply with the family rule and feel lonely.

Until these old ideas or intergenerational beliefs and actions are healed and integrated, you act in accordance with or separate from what the family dictates. Unfortunately by knee jerking your reaction, like the majority of people do, you end up lonely either way. Either the women in the family isolate you and keep you away on some levels, or you comply with the family rule and put apart an aspect of your being. This allowing of the separation perpetuates personal, family and societal loneliness. You or another you may know may have experienced a situation where what the generations did before was so powerfully impressed on the current generation that individuals either acted out, got depressed, left the area or complied with resentment quiet or not. All of these actions are part of the dynamic of the lonely soul. See, this person wants to be connected to and cared about. This person compromises who they are and what they are here for in order to be connected to something or someone. Are you willing to compromise who you are to be connected to another?

This can seem straightforward and almost obvious. What goes with this is the power of emotion and connection itself. Just like in certain compounds in chemistry the bond and the power and charge of the bond can greatly affect the stability. As in families, the power of the bonds can greatly affect someone's connection, disconnection, loneliness, or sense of love. It is not noble to chide or disconnect another from the family in the name of love. For many people intergenerational transmission of pain is a real and powerful source of loneliness. Many people are unaware that there is such a thing as intergenerational transmission of pain which makes it so they continue to act in ways that perpetuate the historical loneliness not only into their current lives but on into the future for themselves and the generations to come. I invite you to join me in taking a stand and being the ones that allow the buck to stop so that you can free yourself and those around you from the insidious infection of pain and loneliness that has been passed down knowingly and unknowingly.

Stress

Stress is the last area I will cover in this chapter as far as the causes of loneliness. Stress has many definitions and many experiences for each person who would even hear the word. For the purposes of this text, stress is seen as any resistance or pressure put on your system mentally, emotionally, physically, spiritually or socially that can cause a separation from your source. As I mentioned before, medical diagnoses that confound our support system can be a sign of stress. In addition to the stress of the medical situation, the lack of peer ability to be supportive is another form of stress. Unfortunately, many people use avoidance as a way to deal with stress which continues to perpetuate loneliness in themselves as well as others in their lives.

The stress of being alone can also create additional loneliness. A sense of independence or entrepreneurship, can lead to loneliness in the professional world. Many times, I have heard the comment from others in response to my vision "that's a good idea for you". It can be understood that phrase to mean that the person who heard the idea wants to continue to maintain distance while acting supportive. That mixed message and in the inability of the listener to speak authentically can easily affect your sense of connection to others. You may believe that the primary people in your support system are able to support you when in fact they are unsure and unable to be clear about their support intentions and abilities. You may have people in your life that tell you they support you yet their actions are different than you expect. This kind of stress creates a sense of loneliness within you largely because those people that are important to you remain a step or two away or distress creates loneliness in them because they are unable or unwilling to connect with you. Either way, both people are impacted by stress and loneliness as root causes of disconnection in their relationship.

When loneliness and stress come together in intense ways; it is very easy to see how many people reach out to the wrong people in an ineffective manner to attempt to fill a void that cannot be filled with human action. You could see this as going to empty wells to get water.

Melissa's Story

Melissa is going through a very stressful time in her life. She is graduating from high school and is trying to figure out what to do next. Melissa has acceptance letters to three colleges and she also feels pressure to help at home with the family business. Melissa's parents tell her to do what makes her happy. She is struggling with the choices in front of her. Melissa is feeling such high stress that is largely internally generated that she cannot see some important factors that could make her decisions easier. Melissa tends to be hard on herself and doesn't give herself room to change her mind. Adults in her life are encouraging and she keeps getting more frustrated. Melissa isn't sleeping at night very well and she is increasingly short tempered, even with her loyal and gentle dog.

Melissa attended a seminar about college life and how to deal with the stress of change. She secretly did not think it applied to her but she went because her boyfriend was going. Melissa thought the least she could do was to support her boyfriend who seemed to have it all figured out. Melissa heard ideas that she never considered. She ended up with many moments of clarity and good ideas for solutions for her dilemma. She never would have guessed this but it happened.

Melissa took notes and later talked to her boyfriend about her ideas for a solution to her stress and growing loneliness over these big life decisions. By the end of the day, Melissa had a viable plan to move forward. Her stress was reduced over the next days and weeks as she began to take action based on her plans. Melissa noticed a conspicuous absence of loneliness as the stress level dissipated. She then realized that she feels lonelier when under stress.

For Melissa, her correction was a connection. The connection was within her yet was sparked by an unsuspecting person teaching a seminar. Melissa's success in eradicating loneliness caused by stress is in her action following the awareness. By remaining connected to her mission and her action plan, Melissa uses feedback and input with focus. Melissa's temperament of kindness and compassion returned and she was no longer upset with herself for yelling at her dog. She is able to enjoy the happiness and success that comes with good decisions and actions.

Conclusion

The causes of loneliness can be found in many areas of life and across cultures and age groups. The common denominator is some form or sense of disconnection from self and consequently others. Once this disconnection takes hold, increasing problems begin to manifest and you are feeling not only lonely but also misunderstood and even embarrassed for having the problem to start.

Extroverts may have significant challenges identifying some of these causes. This culture strongly reinforces extroversion so many who are extroverts experience the cause of loneliness in different ways than their introverted counterparts. It is possible to be lonely in a crowded room. Being disconnected from self and purpose is the common aspect of the many causes of loneliness.

Chapter 3

Effects of Loneliness

An effect is a change that is a result of an action or other cause. Loneliness causes many challenges. We have looked at a few of them. There are innumerable effects of loneliness both to the person, family and to the community at large. Reflecting on the effects of loneliness on the human condition, I am overcome with a sense of quietness. The effects of loneliness are obvious in those people who have lost the sparkle in their eyes. Most of the time people who begin to work on themselves have some sort of inner disconnection along with flatness in their eyes. Often they may experience agitation or upset and they express a level of hopelessness and helplessness. You might notice pale skin, flat eyes and affect, as well as a conspicuous absence of authentic smiles. As we move forward together looking at the effects of loneliness, take some time for yourself. It is always good to self-reflect on how anything that impacts you affects you. It is especially important as you read this text, to honor your journey and honor your life experience. Know that loneliness affects all people.

Self-harm

Self-harm comes in many forms. There is the obvious self-harm of inflicting wounds or cutting oneself that all of us can see. Have you ever been so upset with yourself or so frustrated or so angry that you hit yourself? This is a form of self-harm that is extraordinarily common among people who have high intelligence and who are highly sensitive. Self-harm can come also in the form of ignoring our physical welfare by consuming foods that we know are bad for us. This would be when you are told that a certain food could harm you and you continue to consume it anyway. Self-harm also comes in the form of being self-deprecating in your thoughts. Because your thoughts are things, by harming yourselves with your words, both internal and external, you end up creating more pain and a deeper sense of loneliness. When you are feeling lonely and are disconnected do you say things to yourself that if you were to say them out loud you would be appalled? This is ultimate of self-harm. Every single thing you say to yourself is registered in your body; therefore saying things to yourself about yourself that are harmful is an exquisite source of additional pain and a deep-rooted sense of loneliness.

Self-harm also comes in the form of choosing dangerous people or staying in a situation that you know is harmful. Examples here would be dating people or associating with people who are not in alignment with your highest good, like the high school girl who dates the "bad boys". Staying in harm could also mean you choose to remain in an abusive situation where you are physically hurt in order to avoid the effect of being lonely. The paradox here is that in order to survive while experiencing trauma and abuse, you must close yourself off from your feelings and other avenues for support. This harm is a form of loneliness. What you think is helping you feel less lonely or is helping you not deal with loneliness is in fact creating a deeper sense of loneliness and separation. Truly, you must look at this from a vantage point other than linear perspective. All of the causes from which loneliness impact humanity are much greater than you realize.

Do you harm yourself by holding onto beliefs that no longer serve you? Do you harm yourself by shrinking and playing small? Do you harm yourself by continuing in unhealthy ways that you must keep secret? These are all important questions and important ideas to pay attention to as you engage on your growth process.

Addictions

Another effect of loneliness is addictions of all kinds. I named addiction also as a cause of loneliness. I believe addiction is a cause and an effect of loneliness. Because the disease of addiction isolates the user from support or peers, it mimics the domestic violence cycle. Many professionals would say that addiction can also mimic the signs and symptoms of post-traumatic stress disorder. Often, people who are feeling especially lonely will engage in more risky addictive behavior with a faster progression toward their own demise. In this way addiction is the cause of the initial loneliness and it is the effect of the ongoing perpetuating loneliness. Addiction here could be from anything like drinking alcohol to being addicted to self-pity or fear or other patterns of behavior that are causing trouble in your life areas.

Isolation

Another effect of loneliness is a sense of isolation. I describe isolation as a kind of emotional prison that has real walls that keep the person from being able to engage or connect with other humans. When an animal is in isolation, it does not thrive. Failure to thrive syndrome is what happens when an animal that is meant to connect with another of its species is unable to do so. I believe this is why many people are so attached to their pets. By connecting to your dog or your cat that sense of isolation or loneliness can be diminished. I also believe that using your dog or your cat or another pet in lieu of another human connection offers a false sense that the loneliness is less than it truly is. Humans are meant to be connected to other humans in respectful healthy ways. Isolation is not natural to humans. My labradoodle is with me right now. We are connected but to believe that petting her as I write this book would ease a sense of loneliness only scratches the surface of the depths that loneliness can reach. My dog is a great companion and we have a lot of fun yet she cannot fill the need to inner and outer human connection. Connection with other humans remains vital for healthy functioning.

Depression

Depression is also an effect of loneliness. When people are disconnected from others, they tend to go within and perpetuate the cycle of loneliness. Depression can come in many forms and from many causes. One common understanding is that depression of any kind has the propensity to be the effect of loneliness. If a human is left alone and isolated for a period of time, depression is a real possibility. Even folks who report feeling lonely when around other people can experience the real power of depression.

Candy's Story

Candy was always the life of the party in college. She met people easily and she was one of the popular girls in her new school. Candy was raised in a small town. She made excellent grades and she was well known. Candy went away to college excited for her new adventures. The college she picked was only a few hours from home but was quite large in area and number of students.

Candy studied often and she was dedicated to her school work. She knew that she would have to work hard to be recognized as she was choosing a difficult subject. She could handle it though. Over time, Candy was going out less and less, not meeting any new people. She had her roommates and that was enough for her. Candy began to miss her home town and her family. She missed her dog and waking up to her every morning.

After a few months, Candy was having a hard time sleeping. She was under eating then over eating. Candy was struggling with feeling sad and depressed. Candy was a great actress and she never let anyone see her cry or even look the slightest sad or depressed. Everyone thought she was doing well and excelling because her grades were excellent.

One day, Candy went to the school counseling office to get help. She figured that she could go talk to someone who would tell her that she was normal and no one would have to know. After the appointment, Candy cried all the way home. "I have depression, I am so alone and isolated" she lamented. The school counselor shared some actions for Candy to take which would help her feel better. They scheduled another appointment to be sure that Candy was implementing the suggestions and to be sure she was feeling better. Candy shared what happened with her roommates.

Candy admitted to feeling lonely for a long time and was ignoring it so her friends would not think less of her. Candy learned a valuable lesson that day. Depression is a real problem and it can come when she lets loneliness and isolation take over her life. Candy now takes action to relieve any loneliness so that the depression remains no longer an issue.

Chronic Defeatism

Being a defeatist or pessimist is an effect of loneliness. The more chronic the person is defeatist in their thinking their words and their behaviors, the more severe the loneliness is when they look within. When you look at your own life and see negative thinking or pessimistic defeatist comments, you will see the sense of loneliness. Many times this kind of loneliness is not verbalized. It simply shows up as a strong desire or urge to get around another person. One thing to remember is that whenever you feel a very strong urge to try to connect with someone even if it's not healthy, loneliness is at the core of that motivation.

Self-deprecating and self-defeatist comments and actions are real effects for people who are lonely. Often you may express apathy, anger or resentments and these come out as being defeatist. Depending upon the strength of the wall you have built around you, you may be able to see the loneliness. Often this takes some work to see this effect. What are some ways that you have been negative or self-defeatist that you can see are related to feeling or being lonely?

Anxiety

Another effect of loneliness that is quite common is anxiety. Some anxiety is due to a lack of oxygen in the system, some anxiety is a situational response to an external stimulus, some anxiety is a situational response to an internal stimulus, and some anxiety becomes labeled as a form of mental illness. I have also seen anxiety or the expression of anxiety manifest while going through a significant life change. When you are experiencing loneliness and you are nervous or upset; reaching or grasping outward to connect to someone can ease the anxiety symptoms for a time. This feeling of anxiety is often described as loneliness which becomes the fuel for the action of reaching out. In a world where you are reinforced for looking outside of yourself for your sense of well-being and sense of who you are, loneliness surfaces. When you look outside of yourself for the solution, anxiety is often the result. This is a perfect setup for the pharmaceutical industry to continue to grow with anti-anxiety medications.

In most cases simply slowing down helps you find purpose and often completely reduces or eliminates your experience of what you may call anxiety. Increasingly over time you can see how anxiety is an effect of loneliness and as you heal your own loneliness any sense of anxiety you might be experiencing would be greatly diminished or completely eradicated. This is a level of freedom that transcends words other than excitement and enthusiasm.

Poor Relationships

For many of you loneliness has led to poor choices in your associations with people or relationships whether it is with a group or a work situation. You may have at some point let loneliness or the fear of being lonely drive you to associate with people or put yourself in situations that you wouldn't otherwise do in order to somehow diminish or avoid the feeling you so desperately don't want. Your mind often will play tricks on you telling you that loneliness is bad or there is something wrong with you.

Being alone and being lonely are two completely different issues. Being alone implies that in human form your physical being is alone; without another in close proximity. For example: I am in my office writing this book and I am alone. This does not necessarily mean that my experience is loneliness. Rather, my time spent alone writing and creating is very fulfilling and joyful.

Loneliness means that you are not connected on a spiritual way which helps you live out your purpose. With this definition, I am not lonely at all in this moment. I know that sharing things that I think in written form is part of my purpose so being alone to write this book for you is being on purpose. Loneliness is not part of my reality today even though I am alone physically.

Sadly many people who are alone believe that being alone is also loneliness. These people tend to reach outside of themselves looking for something in all the wrong places. Sometimes simply clearing up the definitions and understanding what your beliefs are around them will free you from the self-imposed human ignorance.

Poor relationships are another effect of loneliness. You may have remained in a relationship work or personal or have engaged in some type of relationship with the motive to not feel lonely anymore even when the relationship was not one that was good for you. This is where the seduction and potential addiction to self-destructive activity can take hold of a person. The fear which causes the loneliness keeps the loneliness going and then the poor choices in people creates more fear that then creates more loneliness and the cycle continues ever stronger ever deeper. This is a major problem in our society. Have you ever made a compromised choice regarding your relationships as an effect of being lonely or being afraid to be lonely?

Self-sabotage

Self-sabotage is the last effect of isolation that we will examine in this chapter. Self-sabotage comes from the inherent and deep fear of success. Many people have the belief that self-sabotage comes from the fear of failure. In my experience, it is the fear of success. What comes with success that scares most people into sabotaging themselves? Many people in our society today and maybe even you at times have felt an aversion toward increased responsibility or accountability. It is the increased responsibility or role that comes with success that most frightens people into self-sabotage. This self-sabotage is often other than conscious and you may not be immediately aware of this dynamic. Loneliness often is part of the sabotage that happens. Some people believe that to be successful means they have to be lonely. You've heard it said that *it's lonely at the top*. Well this certainly is not true. If you hold that belief consciously or unconsciously, as you grow and evolve and become more successful that fear of being alone at the top could very easily be the loneliness trigger that causes you to tear down your beautiful creation.

Loneliness and separation are major culprits in the self-sabotage areas of your life. Look at places where you were going along just fine, doing the next thing, doing the right thing and for reasons then known or sometimes unknown to you, you begin to tear down the good in your life. This self-sabotage is a result of loneliness, it is a result of the chronic unconscious belief of separation.

We have covered several different effects of loneliness in this chapter. We have looked at self-harm, addiction, isolation, depression, chronic defeatism, anxiety, poor choices in people and relationships, and self-sabotage. All of these effects of loneliness will surface in your life if loneliness is allowed to take root. All people at different times have experienced all of these and more as part of the human condition of loneliness. The idea that humans require connection to other humans is attractive yet challenging at the same time. You may through intergenerational pain or previous history struggle with authentic communication or connection to others. You may be lonely whether you are talking about it or not.

There are those people with charisma and the character that would have you believe that by a happy smile or a funny joke that they are less lonely, this is often far from the truth. If you are a deflector or someone who lives off of the other people around you being distracted by your personality and charisma, you might want to take a few deep breaths here and look within and allow yourself the gift of some inner honesty for what it is that keeps you in a pattern of separation from others. Authentic laughter and humor and jokes are not distracting and do not rely on charisma to put the listener in a kind of trance so that they do not see the depth of what is happening with you.

Conclusion

I want to remind you that there are many more effects that I have not listed. This book would be too cumbersome to list and speak about each one of them. Know that at the root of many emotions, experiences and beliefs that are disconnecting is a kernel of loneliness. Any time you are disconnected from your true essence and your true purpose, loneliness is the culprit. It is time to be free enough to determine what is going on with you and then take the action that will serve your highest good and thus the highest good of all people. You might want to take some time now and note any other effects of loneliness that are currently or historically prevalent in your life. This way as you move forward in this book and you approach the solutions and the cure for loneliness, you will have the opportunity to look at each one of your own challenges for your own personal and unique solutions.

Chapter 4

Consequences of Loneliness

Just as there are effects of loneliness there are consequences that run the gamut from very small or negligible to large and daunting. From low self-esteem and poor relationships to violence and unrest to slow recovery times and ultimately suicide; each person comes face-to-face with the consequences of loneliness within as well as in those around them. The importance of low self-esteem, poor relationships, violence, suicide and the like as results of loneliness impact our society on every level. In this chapter we will explore some of the important and relevant consequences of loneliness evident in society on the day to day basis. Consequence for this text refers to *importance or relevance* of something rather than the more popular definition of the effect or result though it does encompass the ideas at times.

As you read, you may want to make note of areas of your life that are similar or not similar to these areas. There are a multitude of consequences of loneliness. This is not intended to be a comprehensive list.

Low Self-esteem

Low self-esteem and an impaired self-concept are profound and deeply rooted in loneliness. When you suffer from the ongoing belief of being unworthy or somehow not measuring up, low self-esteem is often how you might describe this experience. When you feel isolated or alone and you are disconnected from your purpose, your self-esteem and your belief in yourself begins to diminish day by day. If you are suffering from a diminished appreciation or valuation of your own inherent beauty and worth, then low self-esteem is one of the consequences that you too are paying for loneliness. When you are lonely and not in contact on a day-to-day basis with your true essence, somewhere along the line you have placed a barrier or wall disconnecting parts of you from you. Often times these barriers or walls can be interjected into our world without conscious awareness of the devastating long-term consequences. The more isolated and lonely and disconnected from your purpose that you are, the more likely your self-esteem and your ability to accurately describe or have confidence in yourself suffers.

Jill's Story

Quite some time ago, I helped a professional woman who came to me with what looked like a full life. She had many friends a successful nursing career and activities in many areas of her life. She reported that her self-esteem was "in the gutter". She would cry and share with me the darkness and the depth of her loneliness. Part of her challenge was that on the outside others saw her one way and she felt completely differently. When she would reach out to her friends they would marginalize her experience based only on superficial activities. As you can imagine, this response from her friends further negatively impacted her self-esteem and made it so she felt more and more isolated. Her loneliness and disconnection from who she was on that core level grew over time.

By the time this talented woman came to me, she had the secret belief that she was somehow not worthy. As we spoke, she shared a family history of dysfunction and isolation with trauma as a young child. She reported having worked therapeutically on the trauma damage yet never completely feeling like she belonged anywhere. The sense of aloneness for her has been so pervasive that though she had done a lot of work on herself the idea that someday she could not feel lonely anymore seemed somehow out of reach. This talented woman lived with this chronic low self-esteem and inferiority complex because she held the belief that the loneliness could not be healed. As we worked together and I showed her some ways to help herself reconnect with authenticity, she rapidly began to see the beginnings of a new way of life. Jill was very willing to try new things and she was willing to work with how she was thinking about herself. This made it easier for her to engage in activities that would connect her not only to herself but to others and to her source.

One day I received a telephone call from Jill and it was unexpected. I thought that because she was calling on a Sunday afternoon that something profound was happening or had happened. The moment I heard her voice I realized the profound nature of her calling on a Sunday. It had to do with a breakthrough. You can imagine that my heart jumped for joy rather than holding my breath wondering what could've happened. As I listened to her tell the story, she expressed the power of the moment when she felt connected to herself really for the first time. Disconnection happened the night before. She was doing her homework and being open to making changes. She reported that she had a glimmer of hope that she did have value and worth and that loneliness had robbed her life experience for about 35 years. Then she became more and more excited almost to the point where it was hard to understand her because she was speaking so rapidly.

She shared that when she woke up on Sunday morning and went outside into her yard to have some tea on her patio; she realized that she could see color and experience her life much more vividly, almost like "surround sound and high definition". She was so elated that she could actually experience and feel her life for the very first time. She said: "I am finally connected. Finally that haunting loneliness of not being worthy has been uprooted and replaced by one of value and worth. Thank you so much." We talked for some time and she offered her gratitude. I reminded her that it was her willingness and her effort and focus that came together to free her from the previous darkness of loneliness.

When you connect fully to whom you are and what you're here to do, any shred of loneliness within you dissipates. The goal is to be aware that something as common as low self-esteem comes from a deeper cause that is prevalent in this world. To continue to move into your own freedom and your own purpose and mission, this kind of awareness is paramount.

Poor Relationships

Another consequence of loneliness is poor relationships. When people are driven to seek out or remain in poor relationships because of loneliness or the fear of loneliness, they are choosing a difficult stressful way of living. To allow the seed of loneliness or the seed of fear of loneliness to color your decisions about relationships, you set yourself up for severe consequences as a result. The darkness of fear allows it to grow and soon the poor relationships could take over your life.

Loneliness and the isolation that is part of loneliness attract poor relationships. Often there are people who prey on others who appear lonely or act from fear of being left alone. This desperation is seen by the predators and soon you find yourself in a harmful, poor relationship. This is often a default that keeps happening until you learn the lesson and begin to heal the loneliness and the pain associated.

These poor relationships can be any type of relationship from a family member, employer, acquaintance, lover or co-worker. If you reflect on your poor relationships, you will be able to write the names. Look at the patterns of the relationship itself. Most likely, loneliness or an associated fear or pain response played a significant role in you being in the relationship. This Cure will help you transcend these patterns.

Dysfunctional Interactions

All kinds of dysfunctional interactions are a hallmark for someone who is experiencing loneliness. Often people who have loneliness are desperate to connect. The illusion is that if I connect outside of me to another person, place or situation; I will then feel whole. Then again that is the illusion. The truth is you *must connect inwardly* to who you are in order to heal the loneliness. Whether other people are aware of the difference or care about the difference is not important now. However, looking for love in all the wrong places will lead you down the path of further darkness and further dysfunctional relationships.

Because so many people have difficulty with loneliness on multiple levels, relationships can get out of whack rather rapidly. The power and healing of the relationships that you have, yields the ability to free yourself from the pain and discord of loneliness wreaking havoc in your relationships. Still though, other people may or may not be freeing themselves from their own loneliness. You may have to either teach another, or distance yourself from those who are stuck in the trance until they free themselves so that you can be free.

Chronic Unrest and Violence

Chronic unrest and violence are very potent consequences of loneliness. Lateral violence is a hallmark of a group of people or culture that is lonely and desperate while choosing to externalize the pain rather than heal. Feeling an inner agitation, you may seek to feel better by focusing on another. This is allowing loneliness to dictate your choices thus creating an ongoing cycle that could continue to harm you and others.

Intolerance, impatience and frustration are signs of unrest within you. Violence can be external in the form of verbal or physical violence. Violence can also be silent as when a parent gives their child the "silent treatment" when they were not compliant with the parent's wishes. Violence can be within the person as in depression signs, indigestion or self-harm in its many forms.

Not only does unrest and violence affect the family or community, it affects each person internally while causing damage physically and mentally. Some of the most insidious violence is mental or emotional in nature.

Longer Recovery Times

Longer recovery times and longer medical challenges are very obvious in people who express being lonely. When you are disconnected from who you are in your essence, it is more difficult to heal and it is more difficult to feel hope and faith and goodness than when you are connected. Often medical personnel will act with surprise when a patient who has support heals faster than someone who is full of fear and upset. This makes the most sense. When you are hopeful and connected to who you are as a healing co-creative agent in your own life, you can transcend what other people may be able to think is true for you. The less lonely you are the shorter your recovery times will be. This is a time to celebrate because nobody wants to be down for long!

Suicide

The consequence of loneliness that strikes deeply is that of suicide. Suicide is one of those things that some people don't want to speak about and some people have felt in ways that are unspeakable because there are no words. Whether someone is spawned into giving up or feels that they have no value and therefore shouldn't be around anymore or had their world crashing on them and no seeming way out, suicide or thoughts of suicide are the consequence of profound loneliness. Being so disconnected and unaware of your powerful purpose can obscure your ability to take action for your welfare. The truth is that out of these dark nights, many people emerge stronger more focused and aware than previously.

Still, the real consequence of loneliness is in the despair so deep that suicide appears to be a viable solution. You may have felt hopeless or helpless or may have been suicidal yourself yet know that there is a way to feel connected again and heal the pain that binds you. You living your personal healing and transformation offers you a real sense of focus and hope.

The consequences of loneliness are far reaching. Many people choose not to deal with this issue because it's everywhere and it seems like that's just the way it's going to be. This is the time in human history to live beyond that limited viewpoint and give ourselves permission to do something differently. Now is the time for us to heal the loneliness that is destroying bright and talented and gifted people every day. Whether these people suffer silently or are in need of some kind of medical assistance, loneliness is a definite darkness that affects many, many, people.

I invite you to take some time now and reflect on your own experience. Reflect on the consequences of loneliness in your life. Allow yourself to see how you've been affected by loneliness. Name the consequences of the loneliness. By telling yourself the truth and looking deeper than the surface you can free yourself from this bondage that may appear to show up in every area of your life.

In the next part of this book, I explain the cure for this loneliness. You will see how it comes together piece by piece to offer you hope, to offer your life, and to offer you abundant joy. I invite you to journal your experiences and to be honest on the deeper levels with yourself; taking a few breaths here and there that are deep enough to help you relax. After all, this is a safe universe and you are here on purpose. You have a purpose. My desire is that you become so fully connected to your authentic self and your purpose that you cannot be distracted and more than that you become a beacon of hope for those people who've not yet found the road to joy and freedom.

PART II

The Cure

Chapter 5

Comprehensive Model

Mental, Emotional, Physical, Spiritual, Social

Chances are that you have been trying to ease or eradicate loneliness by doing one or more actions in one area of your life. You may feel so paralyzed that taking any action seems nearly impossible. Your best efforts given your personal circumstances may not be yielding the results you would like. Take Heart! There is a way out of the seeming dead end.

I invite you to read the entire model and plan before trying to apply the principles. I will explain and define many of the words and concepts as they apply to the plan which may differ from general use of the words. This model comes from many years of working with people and focusing toward results to help them experience a richer quality of life.

Remember that loneliness is very different than being alone. Loneliness impacts all life areas. Disruption in any one or more areas can lead to separation and loneliness. To solve the problem, you must use different strategies than those you used that allowed the challenges to take hold. You will notice that by using this model to cure loneliness that many other challenges will improve or disappear altogether. This truly is a comprehensive model for transformation.

This model includes five major areas of functioning. There are many ways to experience each of these areas as well as their interactions with one another. The following chapters speak specifically to each of the five areas. Read through all the parts before starting. Remain open for your personal solutions. The road to contentment is at hand.

Following each of the five major components there are points to ponder. These are questions that can assist your progress. You may want to have a journal dedicated to this cure for ease in reflecting and noting your progress. Just thinking about things and writing about them yield very different results. Invest in yourself and write some of your thoughts, ideas and emotions. Watch yourself transform from taking small daily actions!

Chapter 6

Mental Clarity

The mental area of this model is critical to the overall implementation. It is our minds that are in charge. An undisciplined mind can and will create one mess after another. Often you are unaware that it is the power of your own thinking that is creating the problems. You use words in your subconscious as well as your conscious. The commercial thoughts, as I refer to them, can create a very different reality than the one your conscious, awake self in thinking about at times. Imagine that every positive thought or word, conscious or unconscious was a white ball. Every negative thought or spoken word is a black ball. Over time, you will quickly be able to determine where your primary thoughts are simply by the ratio of white to black balls in your collection. What you may not realize is that the secret thoughts are also producing balls, not only what comes out of your mouth.

Having mental clarity is essential to a harmonious and contented life. The five areas discussed next will more clearly define aspects applicable to mental clarity.

Belief Systems

The high majority of your belief systems were instilled in you prior to the age of two. Therefore, many of the ways you view and experience the world, the beliefs, are non-verbal. These beliefs have the most power in our daily lives. When you say or act in a way that confounds you, there is an old belief system calling your shots. The good news is that there is a way to change the beliefs that are no longer serving your life and happiness. Nonetheless, old belief systems can show up at inopportune times and with great force. Part of this system is to become increasingly aware of the belief systems that you are using to live by and determine what is serving and what is not serving. This takes honest, self-reflection and a level of curiosity. An "I don't care" type attitude keeps you living out old patterns over and over. This is how you become stuck and the experience of being on a hamster wheel ensues.

To uncover many of your belief systems, you can use the "If... Then..." formula. This is a good starting point. Use your journal to list a few If/then statements. Here is an example: **If** someone is angry, **then** it is my fault. Now, take a few minutes and look within and see what beliefs that may be part of your beliefs that you may or may not currently agree with today. We have beliefs about everything from the laws of nature and human expression to how we operate in this world. Not all beliefs cause problems and challenges. It is the discerning person who takes the time to look within and make adjustments as indicated to experience freedom and Joy. You are that person, I am certain of this fact!

Shame

Shame has its own category for the purposes of curing the loneliness that has you seeking a solution. Shame is the belief that you are inherently no good. Many say it is the statement that you say to yourself: "I am a mistake." I think far too many people have said or still say these hurtful words about themselves. In our popular language today I hear guilt and shame interchanged in describing events or one's actions. Guilt means that you crossed your own boundaries whereas shame means that you hold a belief that you are a mistake. No matter how many mistakes you have made, YOU ARE NOT A MISTAKE. In fact, you are here on purpose with a mighty purpose.

If you have a deep shame language within, it makes it extremely difficult to accept the good life that comes with mental freedom. Shameful people secretly are berating themselves, with the belief that they are a mistake. When good things happen, a person with undisciplined and shame based thinking will often decline or sabotage the good life; thus the cycle of pain, grief and loneliness continues. Shame clouds your thinking and thus impairs mental clarity. You will be able to use this model and the other four areas to help uproot and free yourself from shame and its control in your life.

Self-Talk

What do you say to yourself on an ongoing basis in your own voice? Most people are talking to themselves nearly all day long. Are you paying attention? Are you aware that those thoughts have the power to manifest into your life? Self-talk is key in your success and evolution. If you are cutting yourself down most of the day and then using one or two affirmations, the numbers are continuing to work against you. It is not the affirmations or your desires that are impeding your progress; it is all the contraindicated self-talk. STOP the madness of cutting yourself down and speaking negativity into your life.

Mental discipline and thought discipline are ongoing projects for your growth and process in curing loneliness and achieving Joy that is yours by birthright. Sloppy thinking yields sloppy results. It is easy to have mental discipline when things are relatively calm and you have spent some time in quiet. Add some emotional pressure and stress and your discipline will have the chance to demonstrate your commitment to speaking a higher truth than the common human ignorance around you. This is when you become that perfect agent of change that you are seeking to become in this world. Your heart's desire is the seed of the change agents and your thinking is the perfect catalyst.

What you say to yourself matters. Your brain believes your own voice over all other voices even if the message started with someone else. Is your self-talk supporting you or hindering you?

Power of Words

Your words have creative power. Remember when you were little and did not want to go to school so you told your mother "I'm sick"? You even did a convincing acting job and you got to stay home! Hooray for you. What you did not yet know was that your words had the power to create. When your friends got home from school, you had the idea to convince your mom that you were feeling better only to discover that you were now not feeling well. Your plan backfired, or did it? Your creative power in the words you use has been yours and every human's power for all of time. The issue is that most people are unaware or do not take this seriously.

There are additional factors that impact the manifesting in your world. Emotional intensity and congruency, your ability to receive as well as the beliefs around the words play a major role. All these aspects are intertwined and operate as a collective, without exclusivity or separation.

Take a few days and notice the words you use in your everyday language. Be mindful that all the words you use have creative power. When you say "I love you to death," You may want to begin to restate this love as "I love you in life." I don't think that you meant to speak death over your loved one yet that is what happened. Your brain deals with the words in their literal and vibrational form; not respective of your sarcasm, joking or unknowing. Often, you will be frustrated in your endeavors because you are speaking words that are contradicting your goals without being aware you are doing this daily.

What you are speaking about, you are getting more of every day. Speak about fear and loss and you are essentially calling these to you. Speak about success, contentment and joy, same process is occurring. All words have creative power, what you create is entirely up to you. For increased mental clarity, you want to develop good vocabulary and command of the language. Use your words with precision. In other words, say what you mean and mean what you say.

Thinking Strategies

Thinking strategies are also important for you to be aware of within this mental arena of the solution. How you think is part of your mental self. Do you think linearly as in the scientific method? Do you think spatially? Maybe the thinking strategy you use is a combination of these. There is no wrong strategy, there is your strategy. What is important is your understanding and clarity of your personal strategy. The more aware you are, the more powerful your results.

You may be the one who is the visionary, seeing the big picture and share that picture. You could be the person who is great at taking concise action based on a predetermined plan and set of directions. You may be on who speaks in short, no-fluff language; the "get the job done" style. You may be the one who has to tell the whole story in order to answer a question. You are getting the point, I imagine. The thinking strategy you employ greatly affects your ability to connect with others and thereby begin the healing process from loneliness. A linear thinker alone with many visionaries could be challenged to be connected and soon loneliness could creep into daily life.

Your thinking strategy can morph over time and in different situations. You also have a primary strategy that is most comfortable for you. There is no need to attempt to change your strategy unless it is not working in several areas of life. There is a strong need that you focus on identifying your personal strategies and working within your talents. Begin to see strategies in others, being open to where the synergies take place.

These five aspects that affect mental clarity could be an entire text. For purposes of this book, your awareness and honesty about your thought life play an important role in your use of the model. As you continue by looking at your emotional freedom area, keep in mind that all these aspects impact one another.

Points to Ponder:

1. What is your belief system about contentment? Loneliness?
2. What is your self-talk about your ability to be successful in life?
3. What is stopping you from being mentally happy and free?
4. In what ways are you easily distracted from your goals?

Chapter 7

Emotional Freedom

The emotional area of your life contains the power that causes your actions. Your emotions can cause you to love, fear, purchase things, cry, scream and laugh to name a few things. It is your emotions that ultimately are responsible for many of your actions. Emotions impact your mental and physical experience, both outwardly and inwardly. To experience more freedom and flexibility, you must begin to thaw the frozen emotions and cool the heated ones in order to allow for a flow of life energy through your body.

Feelings are the energy source that tells you that you are alive. The names you use for the energy is simply that, your assigned name. When you call a particular energy depression you are right and if you call that same energy sad, you are also right. The label colors and defines your emotional experience. Labels point toward the energy. It is the energy that is the feeling.

The body bears the burden of unresolved emotions. Grief and anger and fear being held in the body for years can cause many physical ailments and even diseases. Muscle tension can come from anger being held in over time.

Fear can affect your organs. Kidneys are affected by the fears that you hold, consciously and unconsciously. The power of this area includes being able to talk about and process emotions that may be stuck. Fears can cause tension and eventually add significant amounts of stress in the body and mind. These emotions impact every area of your life.

Unresolved Grief

Old pain and unresolved grief impair emotions all the time. Too much old pain and you can be numb to the hurt in yourself or others. Any hurt from an old relationship that is not healed and released causes problems on all levels. You may think it is somehow righteous to continue to hold old grief. Maybe you lost a loved one and you believe that by healing the pain you will forget the person. You hold onto the pain and you end up sick.

Many people wear their unresolved grief like a badge of honor. What they may not be aware of is that this badge will ultimately shorten their life. Do you want to deal with disease and problems because you are unwilling to free yourself from old pain?

You will know the grief is healed when it no longer controls your actions and your emotions do not change when the person or event is brought to your attention. If you think of an old boss and you still feel defiance, pain or anger, the grief is alive in you on some level and is creating ongoing loneliness. You may be holding on to being right yet still the grief and conflict continue to create separation in your life. Do you want to be right or do you want to be happy?

Guilt

Guilt is a natural human emotion. Guilt means that you made a mistake and broke one of your own rules. This is not interchangeable with shame. Guilt is a heavy emotion and can be part of the cause of many physical ailments including cardiovascular events.

Do you have lingering guilt in your thoughts and emotions? How is this guilt perpetuating a sense on loneliness or the fear of being alone? Are you ready to relieve guilt of the driver's seat and begin to make decisions for your life from a contented and grateful attitude and demeanor? Reality is that we all make mistakes. They are just that a *"mis—take"*. When you put perspective on making mistakes, you can begin to reconnect and decrease loneliness in your life. There are many ways to heal and make amends for word and actions for which you experience guilt. The loneliness cure will help clear these blocks away as well.

There are many great ways to heal guilt. Accepting forgiveness and making future changes is vital to your success. Often the one place of forgiveness that is most important is self-forgiveness. Yes, self-forgiveness is very important. Always remember to look within yourself to identify the blocks. These inner blocks are being shown to you in your outer world so you can heal and become free. Each block adds to the loneliness you experience.

Anger

Anger is a secondary emotion. This means that it always comes after another emotion. That emotion is pain. Any form or intensity of pain can fuel anger. Often you will be able to assess your behavior and be able to identify times when you were hurting and it came out with anger. One example might be that you had a headache nearly all day or your back is chronically hurting. You have plans with a friend for the evening and you have been excited to see that person all day, despite the nagging physical pain. At the last minute, your friend cancels. You become very angry and frustrated. This anger and frustration was first the pain of disappointment that you converted into frustration. The ongoing physical pain added to the decreased tolerance and now you are angry.

This is an example of how emotional freedom is necessary if you are to be free from loneliness. Learning how to properly identify and express your emotions adds freedom and happiness. You can then connect more effectively with others and your loneliness meter keeps going down!

Fear

Fear of success is the root of self-sabotage. If you have ever sabotaged yourself, then fear of success is the culprit. By looking inward at your belief systems (mental area) and how the belief systems affect your emotions, you have the necessary awareness to make changes in your life strategies as needed. Maybe your definition of success includes a belief that you somehow have to compromise yourself to be successful, then sabotage is the natural unconscious behavior pattern that will keep the belief system intact, even if the belief system is no longer serving your life.

Fear of failure can underlie and can trigger emotions that create more loneliness and separation from others. In fact, fear of failure impacts most people on many levels. Emotionally, you are impacted by your beliefs about failure and the fears associated with failure. The more fears, the more frozen you may be in this area. The goal is emotional freedom and expression of emotions in a healthy manner.

There are many fears that apply in this area. For emotional freedom to be established and maintained it is important for you to identify the fears that are currently blocking your freedom. Fear of loneliness itself, fear of overwhelm, fear of dying, fear of transitioning from one job to another, fear of moving, fear of water and other existential fears can all block your freedom and fuel loneliness at the same time.

One powerful way to get in touch with your feelings is with your breath. Breathing from your abdomen helps unlock stuck energy. Take time each day to focus on your breathing. Breathe in to the count of six and pause for two counts, breathe out to the count of 2 and pause for 2 counts. Do this for three minutes initially then raise the frequency and duration until you are really breathing fully most of the day. Know that air is your friend and there is plenty to go around.

In conclusion, emotional freedom is vital to your ongoing health and well-being. You and everyone else have emotions that are blocked or thwarted somehow. This part of the model is one that you will revisit often. Your emotional health depends upon your ongoing willingness and ability to release the old walls you previously built for safety. The fear of being free can be a big factor. Look within, what emotional bondage are you holding on to because you are afraid to let it out? Are you afraid of your own emotions? Many people start with simply making friends with their own feelings. The point is to be open and available for you own process. Everyone is different. Comparison is of no use.

Points to Ponder:

1. What grief and unresolved pain is fostering continued loneliness? Are you willing to release this and be free?
2. What scares you about being contented?
3. Do you have any guilt that is difficult to release?

Chapter 8

Physical Ease

Physical ease is a powerful and tangible part of the model. Ease refers to a flow and way of operating that is free of friction and resistance. This is quite different than your physical world being easy. Easy implies that success and connection comes with little or no effort required. For this part of the model, your focus turns to going about your life with a sense of *ease*, no matter how busy you may be at any time. To the extent you have resistance, defiance, frustration or blocks you lack ease. This is an area to investigate to determine what needs to be freed up for your equilibrium to return. There are five primary areas I will address in this section. They are: acute physical pain, chronic physical pain, unhealthy environment, nutrition and exercise.

Physical pain really gets our attention. So many people either brag about being able to handle pain or that they are in pain. I believe humans tend to pay particular attention to physical pain because it immediately impairs our experience and can hamper our functioning within our environment. You may have some form of physical pain that is also playing a role in your loneliness.

There are two categories of pain that I will address in this section. The first to note is acute physical pain. This is an injury or a sharp pain that can come from within or is inflicted on the body. In both cases the length of the pain is short lived even though the intensity may vary.

Chronic pain is the other type of pain. This pain is one that is lingering and has been around for quite some time. Dull or severe, the difference is in the length of the pain impacting the person. Chances are you have one or both of the pains happening for you right now.

Acute Physical Pain

Acute physical pain is also a major factor in our life experience. Pain that is acute really gets your attention. You will normally act to relieve it as quickly as possible. Acute pain causes tremendous stress on the entire system and impacts all areas of your life. An injury is an example of acute pain. Depending upon the severity, there is swelling and inflammation, blood loss, adrenaline and other hormones released to aid the body in many ways. Depending upon the nature of the physical injury there can be emotional pain and fears triggered that also impact the system.

You may start saying unkind things to yourself or even blaming yourself. You may get into blaming another. You self-talk is most likely compromised or the old negativity could become reinforced. After taking the necessary measures to stabilize the body, you can use the loneliness cure to assist you with your reconnection with others. This is how you can head off loneliness from entering your life as a result of an acute injury.

Chronic Physical Pain

Chronic pain carries with it an impact that is often long lasting. It hampers your system in moderating additional pain on other levels or intensities. Have you ever had a headache and kept pushing through? Later in the day, you accidentally stub your toe and you blow up over something that seemed so small. The blow up was the result of your depletion from having to deal with the chronic pain on a subconscious and at times a conscious level for hours. The new acute pain created a breakthrough experience that seems to amplify both pains. This happens to people every day. Chronic pain is nothing to laugh at or diminish in any way. I have worked with athletes who have old injuries that have a chronic residual pain level. You must take this into account when planning your freedom from loneliness and disconnection. As long as your system is mitigating chronic physical pain, it is like a small leak in your tire. Every once in a while that tire will need an extra shot of air. Every once in a while these athletes need an extra healing type relief to help ease or stop the drain for a time.

Unhealthy Environment

Your environment is a major factor in your life and it is part of your physical life area. When your environment at home, work or vehicle is out of alignment or cluttered, it impacts your daily functioning and sense of connection. If you explain your mess or clutter or dismiss it by saying something like "I know where everything is". That's nice and that is not the point. Stagnant clutter produces a type of "stuckness" in other areas of your life. Whether you know it or believe it or not, the truth is that if the energy around you keeps getting stuck, then your life will feel like running through Jello rather than thin air.

Look around your sleeping and work spaces first. Are they free from clutter? When the energy around you slows down or becomes stuck, then you suffer even if you are not yet aware of this. Take some time and de-clutter and rearrange your sleeping area of your home. Dust, vacuum, change the sheets and de-clutter the area. This includes closets, drawers and under the bed. Now, let the air flow, either use a fan, open the windows, something to get fresh air in and have the energy flowing again. Then leave that space for a while. After some time, re-enter that space. You will notice a lighter and freer experience, even if you cannot put words to this feeling. This is the feeling of energy flow. Stuck energy causes sickness of mind and body and soul.

Feeling the transformation of one area will inspire you to continue to methodically cleanse your world of clutter and anything that makes your life force sluggish or stuck. Environment includes your internal physical world.

Nutrition

What you eat, when you eat and from where you eat makes a marked difference in the quality of your life. When you don't feel good or you feel sluggish or heavy, it makes it more difficult to go out and be with others. This is a hot bed for the growth of increasing levels of loneliness. If you don't feel good about yourself physically, then you are more likely to in some way depreciate you in the face of the world. Loneliness then becomes the effect and the perpetuating cause of increasing challenges. Because your goal is to cure loneliness and you are focused on being free, you have the challenge to really pay attention to what you put in your body.

I will not go deeply into nutritional areas. There are many great teachers in this area. I will say a couple things about overriding concepts. If your body doesn't like something, stop eating it. Taking a pill to mask side effects of poor food choices is only causing more problems. Alcohol is a direct numbing agent and poison. Remember the old western movies when they used bourbon to numb the gunshot wound? Well, do you really want your body to have to deal with repeated poisoning in order to keep you alive? When I step back and look at what we call food and how we, as a culture, abuse our bodies, I am amazed at the Creator of these bodies. Your body is constantly undoing your poor choices. This causes stress on the system and can add to your overall challenges in a quiet and insidious manner until it raises its ugly head and you are very ill. Then the acute pain takes over. This pain becomes chronic though you use denial or ignore consequences for a time.

We all can grow and make necessary changes to our diet. This is why this cure for loneliness if a progressive, daily practice without a finish line. All you have to do is make a small change every day and you will see compounded results. More on this part of the cure will be covered in a later chapter.

In addition to food, our body needs exercise. You may require a different type of exercise than your friends. The one universal truth is that everyone needs to move or we will become stagnant and then moving will become increasingly difficult.

Exercise

Exercise and moving your body is a key component in the physical cure of loneliness. Your body is meant to move. Cardiovascular exercise is a dynamic and integral part of reconnecting. On average, it is good to do a minimum of 30 minutes of cardiovascular exercise each day. I am not talking about straining yourself. I am talking about getting up and moving your body faster than sauntering to the mailbox!

Rhythmic exercise is also a key component of physical ease and health. In this exercise, your limbs cross the center line of your body. Rhythmic exercise helps to harmonize the right and left hemispheres of the brain. When your life is out of alignment and loneliness seems to prevail, it is likely that your brain is struggling to balance the hemispheres.

Rhythmic exercise helps this communication and it does not take long to actually feel less disjointed and alone. Examples of rhythmic exercises could be: Tai Chi, Zumba or an aerobic group where you cross center line often, calisthenics, and any activity that crosses your center line. Sometimes I have had children I have been working with do "silly walking" where they make up funny walks and they must have arms or legs cross the center line. They love the silliness and they become more centered and aligned while having fun.

Weight training and resistance training are valuable exercises to help create physical ease for your body. Your muscles are not an extra part of you; rather they are vital to your life and health. Tight muscles do not have ease and your body suffers. Tight quadriceps and tight hamstrings can create all kinds of physical pain for your knees and lower back. Tight muscles in your shoulders and neck can give you terrible headaches. Muscles cramps are your body telling you that they require better attention and focus for their proper functioning. Stretching and relaxation for your muscles are required for a healthy body. A healthy body is required if you want to be able to be connected to others and relieve separation and loneliness.

It is a great idea to use a good certified personal trainer to help you learn proper stretching and proper techniques. Ask around and interview prospective trainers. Make sure that you are comfortable and can remain focused on your goals. I find that having a personal trainer is vital to my focus and success.

You may have an injury or long standing physical challenge that requires expert assistance. Exercise physiologists, corrective exercise trainers, physical therapists can work in tandem with you and your health care team to assist with improving overall functioning. Corrective exercise is specific and works well when done properly. The point is that you can become increasingly physically at ease. Your body has an amazing capability to heal and transform.

It seems part of the chronic physical challenges stem from overall lifestyle. By remembering that getting up and moving while fueling your system properly is part of your freedom, you are empowered to make better choices. After all, physical ease is up to you. It is easier to connect to others when your body works in the way that supports your life.

Points to Ponder:

1. Where are you tolerating or ignoring pain? What actions can you take for healing?
2. How uncluttered is your environment? Are there actions to take to reduce stuck energy?
3. Do you exercise at least thirty minutes daily? How can you create proper exercise for optimal health?
4. What foods give you energy? What foods cause indigestion or lower your energy?
5. Are you drinking at least half your body weight in ounces of water daily?

Chapter 9

Spiritual Assurance

The spiritual assurance part of the cure possesses enormous possibilities. Spiritual refers to your inner connection to your purpose while also being connected to the greater. This is quite different than religion.

Your spiritual nature is profoundly connected to your life's purpose and heart's desire. This aspect of the cure reminds you that you have a personal mission that is trying to emerge through you into the world.

The more connected to this aspect you become, the less loneliness can creep into your life. When you are connected to your essence and purpose, loneliness is impossible. There is no room for emptiness.

It is through your spiritual connection that you attain a sense of belonging and value. This belonging is vital to your happiness and success.

When you are connected to your essence; your perceived value as a human being becomes profound. You can now release the drive to prove yourself by doing. You are a valuable being – this spiritual connection is your assurance. Four aspects of spiritual assurance are pillars in living the loneliness cure. They are: life's purpose, heart's desire, sense of belonging and worthiness.

Life's Purpose

All people have a purpose for being alive. If you want to know what your life purpose is, try not to do it. Your purpose is that thing that keeps showing up. Your spirituality is our connection to your purpose. Around ages 28-32, many people begin to ask questions about life purpose. You may already be asking as well.

Your life purpose remains consistent and your expression of your purpose most likely will change and evolve over your lifetime. If you purpose is related to teaching, this can show up in traditional ways as well as unconventional ways. Your purpose is teaching nonetheless. You may notice shifts and changes in your life. Any sense of loneliness is often a place where your spiritual connection is dim.

To cure your loneliness, your life's purpose must be identified, honored and respected. Using a journal and other areas of this model can help you uncover and attain clarity about your personal purpose. Most often if you are struggling it is because on a deep level you know what your purpose is and you are afraid to acknowledge or share at this time. Disconnection or distancing yourself from connecting to your life purpose is an area where you are the primary one creating the fertile bed for loneliness to grow. You may think you are misunderstood or you cannot be yourself. Both of these are a disconnection from your purpose. Spend time in quiet and look within.

When you initially connect to your purpose, you may feel fear because of not knowing how to do the purpose. Not to worry, you will learn what you need along the way. All you need to do is *say yes* and allow the rest to unfold! Remember; use a journal to assist you in identifying specific trends and ideas. This wil help greatly.

Sandy's Story

Sandy is a talented teacher. Her students love her. She teaches elementary school age and her abilities wow parents and students alike. It hasn't always been this way for Sandy. Last year, she took a year off from teaching. She was unhappy teaching at the college level where she had taught for several years. Sandy shared how she was tired often and was increasingly unmotivated. Her career had seemed to hit a dead end and she was so unhappy. Sandy left the college and swore she wouldn't teach anymore. She got a job in another industry and she loved it. She could use her creativity and was happy once again. She would share how she used to teach but not anymore. Over time at this new job, Sandy was asked to help with new hires. She gladly said yes. Soon, she was the one training new people at her work. She remembers how she loved teaching and why she pursued it in the first place. Sandy wanted to help others become excited to learn and expand their knowledge in creative ways.

Sandy spent some time reflecting and she began to see that she was meant to teach. But why was she so unhappy at the college: she wondered. Sandy shared her observations and ideas with a trusted friend who reflected with her on her career and journey. Sandy wanted to be creative and the college job discounted that part of her mission. Sandy saw the challenge clearly in a time of reflection and decided to look into teaching in a more creative setting.

Soon Sandy found a local magnet school that focused on the arts with elementary aged children. She became excited to share her talents and creativity. Though the transition offered some challenges, Sandy was happy that she was back following her life's purpose. Her heart never changed, even when she left the teaching job at the college.

Sandy thanked her friend for helping her determine how to deal with her discontent. Sandy remembered hearing that your life's purpose won't leave you alone. Now she understood this idea. Sandy reflects now with fondness her journey and how she enjoys her work more fully because of her awareness.

Heart's Desire

What is your heart's desire for your life? I imagine loneliness is not part of your heart's desire. Your heart's desire is that inner urge that keeps inciting you to grow and evolve. Many people do not ever pursue their heart's desire because of fears. You may know what your heart's desire is and are not going after the very thing that connects you to those around you and the greater universe at large. This is a time to put fear in its place and begin to allow the authentic you to emerge.

Your heart's desire is uniquely yours, much like your personal mission. Your heart's desire has many options for expression and what works best is to express your desire in the way that is of service to you and others.

George's Story

George is an ambassador by personality. Many of his friends, family and colleagues say that they have never seen George in a bad mood or mean to anyone. George is a talented man who has high standards. He is fully aware that everyone makes mistakes. He is not a perfectionist. George's desire is to make the world a happier place. George does this by encouraging others and supporting those around him to step forward to be of service. George laughs and freely brings life to any situation.

What George does for a living or any other demographic is not essential as he goes about his day freely sharing smiles and enthusiasm. His heart's desire is being fulfilled everyday as he gives of himself. George is living his heart's desire to be of service to others. There are others who are serving others in a very different manner. Both are equally valid and vital.

Sense of Belonging

All people want to belong on some level. Belonging is a vital part of development. To what do you belong? Start with the obvious; humanity, Earth inhabitant, your gender, place of living, career, church, school, vocation, etc. The deeper sense of belonging that yearns within all people is essential to the spiritual assurance part of the cure. Do you belong?

You do belong. No matter what your thoughts said as you read the question, the answer is yes! Loneliness can create the experience of not belonging in general or specifically. Sometimes you may experience such loneliness that you don't think you belong in your own skin. There are many varying experiences. I am sure you have felt many different examples of belonging throughout your life. Think of middle school and you will have plenty of examples!

Worthiness

Are you enough? Well, of course you are. Have you ever thought you did not measure up somehow and therefore are not worthy or enough? This is a big topic when it comes to experiencing spiritual assurance. Do you deserve to be connected and part of the universal family of humans and other beings?

You are a beautiful being who is a blessing from your inner core self out into the world. How are you expressing your true inner beauty? The power of this cure for loneliness is that you do not have to prove your worth to anyone. You are valuable and this model helps you see your value and connect. In this connection, the loneliness dissipates and is replaced with joy, freedom and excitement for living.

Points to Ponder:

1. Do you feel worthy? Are you enough?
2. Do you know your life's purpose?
3. What are ways to bring forth your heart's desire?
4. Do you feel a sense of belonging in your world?
5. How is your spiritual connection the same or different from your religious life?
6. Are you willing to "say yes" to your life's work?

Chapter 10

Social Connection

Social connection offers a myriad of solutions as part of your loneliness cure. Whether introverted or extroverted, being connected to others is necessary for healthy functioning. The connections may look different yet are equally important for your success. There are three challenges to healthy social connection that I will cover in this chapter. Isolation, social awkwardness and insecurity seem to have profound impact on connection.

Isolation

The first thing being lonely does is isolate you from being connected within and without. Other things that perpetuate isolation include stressful living situations or work environments. This piece of the model is vital to your long term success and happiness. It may also be the most challenging for you to pursue. Introverts or folks with low self-esteem can be more easily afraid to take the risks necessary to move forward.

You may be feeling isolated from others really understanding you. Isolation is not about how many people are around; it is about how connected you are to those that are around. You can be in a room full of people and still feel alone. I'll bet some of you are nodding your heads yes as you read this.

Social Awkwardness

Social awkwardness is something that the social connection part of the plan addresses. You may have some hesitation or you may know others who have challenges in this area. Social awkwardness is common with bright and talented folks. Sometimes they are called "geeks". You can be a geek about nearly anything and this can create social awkward situations. When I was first going to college, I could talk all day about racing sailboats or the weather. I had no other real confidence in any other topics common in my age group. Thus, landing in a big university, only being able to feel confident to talk about sailing and weather, feeling awkward and introverted, social connection in the new arena was very challenging. It was hard for me to even say my name to a stranger, let alone talk about anything in common. This was a hard time for me. Being socially awkward creates isolation and an invisible wall that is often difficult to break through.

Social connection is the glue that helps you expand your freedom into your everyday life. It is through various social connections that you are able to once again transcend loneliness and thus heal the old, lingering pain associated with being alone.

Insecurity

Insecurity is a byproduct of social disconnection as well as being a cause of disconnection. Do you remember being made fun of when you were younger? Did you do the making fun of another? Well, both come from a level of being insecure. The two types handle it differently yet the challenge is similar; being insecure within the peer group at hand.

A sense of insecurity can inhibit social connection. Insecurity can plague even the most suave and confident appearing individual. Often, it is this separation between what is projected and the secret feelings that can keep insecurity alive.

Insecurity seems to stem from an inherent thought or belief that the person somehow doesn't measure up and therefore is not worthy. This can change from situation to situation and person to person. One person may be insecure about being in groups of people while others may thrive. Some people may think that insecurity is reserved for the shy ones. Well, it is not. There are many who are not shy who report being insecure. Many bright and talented people are insecure in social settings while thriving in intellectual pursuits.

James' Story

James seems extroverted, he always smiles and says hello to everyone if they are in yelling distance. He volunteers to speak first in class and he is a natural born leader. He is always in demand for outings and activities with his friends and family. James is an introvert by personality meaning that he re-charges by spending time alone. This is not obvious to his friends. They just see him as this great personality with a great smile and welcoming attitude.

James struggled with loneliness because he had no real friends or confidants that understood his introverted nature. When he would be quiet and maybe on the periphery of an event, many people would judge him as aloof or maybe even stuck up. James wanted to talk to someone, connect with them, about his situation. The challenge is that his friends don't know about this part of James.

When working with James, he shared that he hid his quieter self from his friends for fear that he would not be liked and it would negatively impact his business. In hiding part of his true nature, he disconnected from himself spiritually and then had no authentic connections for support. He was the supporter and encourager and he lamented to me "I want someone to encourage me like I do them. If only they knew that I needed them." James worked on re-aligning himself with his true nature and allowing his friends to see his quieter side.

After some time, James called and expressed being thrilled with his life and relationships. He shared that some people left his life and many more authentic people have entered his life. James said: "Wow, this really works."

Conclusion

When social connection is strong, you feel a sense of being more alive. Your joy is evident in your daily life and relationships. A sense of belonging is central to healthy living. Belonging leads to a sense of community and understanding. When you are authentically connected on multiple levels, being lonely is impossible.

Points to Ponder:

1. Do you currently feel isolated?
2. When was the last time you felt connected to peers?
3. Is social awkwardness part of your life?
4. How do you deal with your insecurity?
5. How do you deal with others' insecurities?
6. How do you know when you are connected in a fulfilling way?
7. What does Multiple Peer Groups (MPG) mean to you? How is this important to your life?

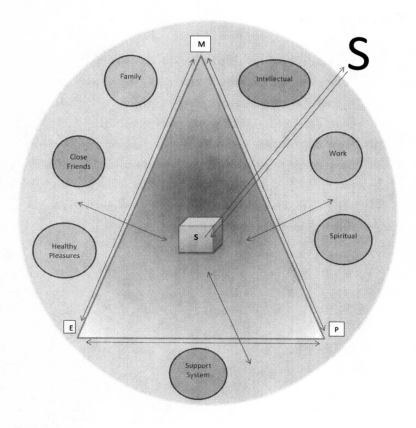

Cooperative Model of Transformation Diagram (MEPSS)

Chapter 11

The Cure Comes Together

Key Aspects of the Model

This program is superb in bringing people to a more fulfilling life experience. In my many years as an instrument for transformation, these concepts come from a combination of formal education and day to day practical experience. To recover means *to feel better.* It is the process you must go through (not around) to effectively change your life for the better. People typically initiate these necessary changes when the pain in their lives becomes so intolerable that there is nowhere else to turn for some form of relief. There is a diagram preceding this chapter for your visual reference.

Along the way, many people turn to anything that will alter their mood. Food, sex, alcohol, drugs, gambling, spending, control, depression and rage to the point of self-destruction are all ways that can be seen around the world. Some of these can be attempts to find relief from the exquisite pain that somehow feels bigger than your awareness. In these dark times, you may cry out for help. Be assured, The Great Universe always answers your prayers, even when you aren't sure there will be a response or that you are even connected. Ha! This is the great humor and paradox of your beautiful spiritual lives and this universe.

The answer always comes. The request is always answered. It almost never comes as we have imagined and usually not from where we think it will come. So many people walk around thinking prayers aren't being answered when in fact they are being answered all the time, not just in the limited ways we think they *should* come. Your biggest and expansive ideas are nothing compared to the magnificence and grandeur of the creative force that sustains all that is within you, in this universe and beyond.

When you make the decision to change your life, there are certain key avenues that can bring about effective transformation when practiced consistently. *Say Yes* is my method of choice used to bring harmony, inner peace, success and balance to life.

When people hear that I subscribe to a holistic approach to transformation, they often assume that my focus is on mind, body and spirit type paradigms. This is a useful way to approach life yet when we are talking transformation; another model must be employed for long lasting results.

For me, transformation means that you are more fully aligned with the Divine flow of the universe and thus experiencing the power and presence of your creative force. Healing transcends our physical limitations and understanding. We must be willing to move beyond limitations and be open to the vast possibilities. Herein are some of the answers you seek.

Getting Started

We start with a circle in the 2 dimensions and a sphere in the 3 dimensions. In practice, this part of the model has no limits. It is deep within you while is also radiates to the far reaches of the universe beyond our limited understanding. This is the spiritual essence and substance of all that is. Plato called it the forms. Some call it God, Lord, Spirit, Universal Energy, Divine Love or Energy. Regardless of your worldview, this energy is in and through all that is and it is greatly affected by our thoughts, words and actions. This spiritual dimension includes our connection to the higher realms of consciousness and it is generally the answer to those questions: "Who am I?" and "What am I here to do in this life?" This speaks to being connected to our purpose!

Many do not realize that we are swimming in this substance from which all is created and we cannot escape this, whether we believe in it or not. It simply exists. In other paradigms, "Spirit" is part of the 3 pronged system. In my experience, Spirit transcends this understanding. It is important to realize that this essence is in all that exists.

The small "s" inside the cube with the 2-way arrows connecting to the larger "S" represents your unique spiritual animation as it relates to the greater. Within each one of us is the longing for connection to something greater. This is most obvious in nature when you might lose track of time while walking on the beach or hiking in the woods. Your spiritual connection transcends time and space and has a 2-way communication with the greater universe. In the diagram, the cube within the triangle is meant to represent that part of us that is part of the greater. We as humans are given dominion and free-will which sets us apart yet all physical form is made of this substance. Thus, all life is sacred on some level.

Within this "circle" is an equilateral triangle. The equilateral triangle is the strongest of all geometric shapes. We want to come from a place of strength rather than weakness or problem. Triangles also represent the trinity of Mind, idea and expression. We are reminded that the spark of the spiritual substance of all that is may be found within each one of us. The sides of the triangle resemble the boundaries much like our skin. This boundary helps us be in the world even though we are not of the world. This is the vehicle by which we travel.

The top apex of the triangle represents the mental aspect of our self. No accident that it is at the top because we as a culture are focused on cognitive functioning and linear tasks. You must be able to think through things to be a success in our Western Culture. This part of the triangle includes your beliefs and self-talk; the way you think and how you process our world. Up to 75% of our beliefs are in place very young in life. Often, when people decide to make major life changes, they run into these belief systems in the form of self-sabotage, fears, nay saying and the like. This area is particularly vulnerable for the linear thinker or the one who relies heavily on cognitive functioning to navigate their environment and the world at large. Many say that the higher intelligence and will power people will prevail.

The bottom left represents the emotional self. Emotions are what move you through life. They create babies, start and end wars, create the memories and experiences of Love and they can protect you when danger lurks. Emotions are meant to be experienced without judgment. Many people hold onto those less desirable emotions and create stories and pain and challenges on all levels. You are often taught and reinforced to see emotions as good or bad which is also greatly limiting. When you stop and consider that emotions are simply energy moving through like a cloud, then labeling them except for linguistic convenience seems curious. The ensuing judgment also limits your life experience. Many people come to me, telling me they are "depressed" when, after investigation, they are "grieving". These are two different things. People can often get stuck in their ideas about how the feeling should feel and how long and intense it should be. But then again, these are belief systems and this is the mental apex! This will be explained as we progress.

The bottom right corner represents the physical self. This includes the body; what you eat, how much exercise you get and other self-care activities. This also includes the environment and our physical surroundings like our vehicles, homes and work or school venues. Healthy physical areas include balanced attention in all of these areas. When you are in harmony in this area, you move with a sense of ease in your environment. This is not to say easy; rather you flow with ease in your day to day activities.

Each and every action or event that occurs in any one of these areas equally affects the other three areas. This is fundamentally critical to the understanding of the interaction of these life areas. Whatever you think or experience mentally, equally affects you emotionally and physically and spiritually; equally.

Where the mind, body, spirit model falls short is the marginalizing of the emotional self. Emotions are what fuel love, war, babies and all of life. The energy of emotion is what tells you that you are alive. In our current Western culture, our emotional experience is often marginalized. This is true especially for men, I believe. The emotional aspect is significant in freeing you from old grief, pain or distorted emotions that tend to impair your life in subtle and not so subtle ways. The other often marginalized area is the spiritual area. I hear people say "I'm becoming spiritual". I ask myself "How can you become more of what you already are by nature?" Yes, we are all here to grow and evolve in these and all life areas. If you are not in touch with an aspect of yourself, it doesn't mean it doesn't exist.

All challenges or addictive related issues come in through your strongest apex of the body triangle. You will note that many projects and challenges first start in the spiritual realms and by the time we are physically affected, the spiritual disconnection has been an ongoing concern. You are often taught that spiritual is religion and one hour a week has you covered. This is simply inaccurate. Your spiritual nature is divinely connected to the greater essence of all that is. Your spiritual nature is meant to evolve and express as an ever expanding emergence of the Good. I notice that a lot of pain in any area of life first begins with a sense of questioning your *enoughness* or value or purpose. Remaining disconnected from your source yields many challenges like exhaustion, fears and various health related concerns.

Albert Einstein said: "We cannot solve a problem with the same thinking that created it in the first place." Einstein had a clear understanding of this. He was an out of the box type problem solver and he employed all his available faculties though he is primarily credited with his intellect. Simply knowing that these four areas interact is nice and the real power of understanding is in the practical application and use of the principles and each one's orientation to the others.

The impact in any one area is experienced equally in the other areas. Thus, if your problem is a mental one; you would be wise to employ another area as the lead to solve the current mental problem. This is not to the exclusion of the mental area, rather to have another area *lead* the solution process. The same process applies for emotional or physical issues. And for all issues, to remember that they first began via a spiritual disconnection and thus healing is called for in this arena. For all projects, spiritual work is a requirement. We are spiritual beings and thus are called to seek spiritual harmony and peace. This speaks to the age old discussion that addresses the question "Are you a human being or a human doing?"

You might be asking about the last "S" in the MEPSS model. Where does that fit in and what does it stand for after all! This last "S" stands for Social. Our human connection is vital for our existence. We are hard wired for human contact and certain levels of intimacy are required for our health and well-being. For your fulfillment and health, your little "S" circles must have within them, like minded beings for each social group. You know that the Divine is found in communion. You cannot heal old wounds alone, though you live in a society that attempts this way of behaving.

Each collective has a spiritual essence that is magnified by their coming together. It is in this coming together that each member receives the benefits of the group. It is also true that you could be brought lower by the ones in the group. This is why discernment is good. In the beginning of making a major life change, it is possible that your *people picker* may be damaged or even seemingly broken. If you have made poor decisions with choosing who to let into your life, your *people picker* is not tuned up! Take solace in the knowing that with work and attention, you will improve. The goal is to have multiple social or peer groups. You have peers at work or school, peers in your family, peers in your sporting activities, intellectual peers, spiritual peers, emotional peers, aesthetic peers, and intimate peers. Each group will vary in size. What matters is to assess regularly how these are working and are they serving your highest good; being ever mindful that your highest good may not be immediately obvious.

Each member of each group has the same energy dynamic happening within themselves, the group and the Creator. There is a synergy that happens as rapport and connection are established and maintained. There truly is power in numbers. The power is in the magnification and focus of the creative energy of the universe working in and through each member. This coming together is inspiring and amazing! We really can do more as a united team than we can do alone. Synergy makes it so.

PART III

Your Life Transformed

Chapter 12

Living the Cure

How to Practice for Authentic Success

There is no finish line! So often your linear thinking brain will try to find a destination or finish line and there is no such destination. The MEPSS model is a paradigm for ongoing personal and cultural evolution. There is no finish line and you are not behind or ahead of anyone or yourself for that matter!

It is time to look at your life and personal growth from the multigenerational view. As the craftsman of the great cathedrals, you will not be done in your lifetime. Your mission is to do your best with love and compassion, knowing that your work will inspire and serve untold numbers of others. The greatest way to immortality is to teach what you know.

There are two ways of living happening within you simultaneously. First is the linear way which helps you with daily problem solving. This is necessary for your functioning with tasks that range from driving to balancing your checkbook. Second, is the circular or higher dimensions which is used for your personal evolution. This is also your spiritual or life's purpose. Here you address life from a feeing or intuitive point of view. You might call it your "gut" feeling.

You may get the linear idea of where you are heading and say to yourself: "I'll figure it out." Or you may attempt to go underground and "comply" with your situation. These do not work in the long run. In reality they are convenient and seemingly noble excuses used to avoid living a full and rich life.

On your journey, there are many sign posts or significant life events. Your mission is to use both your linear and your circular or intuitive aspects in concert. Willingness leads the way to your freedom from loneliness and disconnection.

Your willingness goes a long way in re-aligning your life and in connecting to others and yourself. You must be willing to do things differently, practice new thinking, words and actions. Not always will you have to make the changes you fear. No matter your personal situation, nothing will change for you unless you are willing to do something different.

Each day set your goals and actions for each life area. Spend at least thirty minutes daily focusing on each of the five areas. This means that you dedicate thirty minutes each day to your mental, emotional, physical, spiritual and social well-being and growth. You may want to create a method to document your goals, actions and progress. Be always mindful that all areas affect the others. What you do in one area will impact the others. This is where the power of this model can help you on many levels to be content and free.

It may be challenging to identify specific actions to assist you in living this MEPSS model. I will share with you text from my book *How to Quit Anything in 5 Simple Steps* that delineates actions. I trust this will be helpful. I include a place for you to add your personal ideas.

MEPSS Examples:

Mental: lectures, reading, interviews, documentaries, informational television, belief system identification, quality conversation, learning new ideas about topics you enjoy or wish to have increased understanding of, using tuning forks

Emotional: sharing true feelings and emotions with a trusted other, learning varied expressions of feelings and intensities, breathing fully, safe hugs, art, dance and movement, sound/ vibrational healing

Physical: aerobic exercise, rhythmic exercise, yoga, cleaning out clutter from home/office/car, breathing from diaphragm, weight-training, eating based on body's requirements, self-love and self-care, gardening, staying hydrated

Spiritual: meditation, quiet time, prayer, time with others seeking connection to their purpose, engaging in activities that are ultimately fulfilling your heart's desires, being kind/generous/ compassionate to self and/or other, gardening

Social: time with like-minded group, personal conversation with friends or acquaintances, social group, conversation following another activity like exercise or other gathering, any connection with others that is helpful rather than draining or harmful

You may want to list these ideas and any additional ideas on the next page or in your journal. This will be a nice ongoing reminder of the powerful solutions you have at your fingertips.

Your Personal MEPSS Examples:

Write what your personal MEPSS ideas are to explore.

Mental:

_____

_____

_____

Emotional:

_____

_____

_____

Physical:

_____

_____

_____

Spiritual:

_____

_____

_____

Social:

_____

_____

_____

Be willing to try anything once or twice as long as it is not hurting yourself or another. You must use discernment, not fear, as your guide. Frequently what your best thinking wants to rule out often holds some key ingredients for your growth and personal transformation.

Chapter 13

Connection is the Correction

The Power of MPGs

Multiple Peer Groups (MPGs) are essential for happiness, health, success and overall life satisfaction. Establishing and maintaining multiple peer groups is where most people begin to experience real lasting connections and freedom. This is when authentic change and transformation are probable, not simply possible.

The old notion of you are half and the other person is half and together you make a whole is not only outdated but clearly not helpful. Maybe it makes a nice visual in ceremony or in conversation, but the effectiveness of this paradigm is old news at best. Would you want any relationship with only a half of a person? Would you want to aspire to being only a half of a person? I think not!

In this new paradigm, you are encouraged to become more fully you each day and to become in relationship with others who are allowing more of their authentic selves to show up each day. Allow yourself to take a few deep breaths and connect with your own inner power and goodness. Now, allow this personal power to shine. As you feel the smile come across your face, the real you emerges.

Peer groups are composed of those people who are common to the particular group. Examples of peer groups include: work, school, family, spiritual or religion, support groups, sporting team mates, intellectual and exercise to name a few. One person can be in more than one group at a time. The idea is to have a group that identifies with each major aspect in your life.

If you want to discuss a topic related to your sport/recreation, you would seek out a member of that group. It would not be effective to seek out a member of your spiritual group to speak with regarding a sport specific topic. As much as they may care and want to listen, they are not best suited for rapport in the topic. By matching peer group with desired outcome, you are able to attain better results and thus better relationships.

Personally, MPGs can serve your life on many levels. For example, when you want to talk about philosophical topics and ideas, you have a peer group for that topic. Do not attempt to talk to a recreation buddy from one peer group about deep philosophical matters; rather speak to your recreation peers about the intricacies of the sport. Additionally, your philosophical peer may know little about the same recreational activity so the connection is as strong as it could be.

There is always the potential for crossover within various connections. The point here is that having a peer group from many areas of life allows for real connection. Being personally connected with others as well as within is vital to your overall health and well-being.

Business owners and entrepreneurs are susceptible to loneliness stemming from social isolation. It is challenging to establish a peer group when you are running your business. Not only are there unique demands but there are no peers in your office so you must invest in the action needed to create a peer group with other business owners or trusted business advisors. Loneliness is common with free thinking people, you may want to evaluate this aspect of your life as to determine how you are doing with maintaining healthy peer groups that support your vision and goals.

The social aspect of your life is a key component that brings together and harmonizes the mental, emotional, physical and spiritual areas. Having connection with self and others reduces regrets, we mature and become wise. This is an important part for you introverts! Introverts connect with others differently than extroverts. Comparison is futile.

An introvert can be open and social and if real connection isn't happening, he/she may feel lonely, alone, even with others around. No matter your personality style, MPGs are a key for your success on the deeper levels of life.

What are your primary peer groups? Who would you place in these groups? Chances are that you have various people that fit into the groups. The point is to have clarity about who to go to for connection in a given area. This also helps you determine if you are the right fit when someone comes to you for something. Take some time and look around your life. Copy or complete the chart to help you identify your peer groups. Here is an example.

Table 1

Inner Circle	Family	Recreation	Friends	Support	Spiritual	Work
Sally	Bradley	Elizabeth	Carol	Harriet	Dale	Maggie
Joe	Rachael	Charles	Tina	Kelly	Fred	Jenny
Melvin	Betty	George	Joe	Chris	Laura	Rita
Alyssa	Melanie	Lisa	Samantha	Rose	Sue	Molly

Multiple Peer Group Example

There can be, of course, more than 4 people per group and there can also be less than 4 per group. It is important to know who is where and who transcends the one group into more than one group prior to needing the people. When emotions are high, it is much more difficult to make good decisions. You will tend to reach toward what is familiar even if it is detrimental. Going to an empty well looking for water over and over is the sign of a significant problem. Having proper perspective in advance helps change your history of looking in all the wrong places to get your needs met, especially the emotional and physical ones.

Now create a chart for your life:

Table 2

Blank Table for reader completion

MPGs are vital for an overall sense of being alive. If you are lonely and isolated now, realize that this process takes some willingness, time, patience and open mindedness to develop and maintain. Peer groups are fluid and keep changing. The boundaries aren't rigid in the everyday sense. The important piece to remember is that when you have a real need for connection, it is best sought in the corresponding peer group.

Chapter 14

Intergenerational Healing

Intergenerational transmission of pain refers to the passing down of unresolved pain. This cascading pain energy continues to infect a family until someone with the courage to stop the transmission starts to heal. Most often, the person who begins to heal is not aware of these phenomena and thus is not aware of what they are taking on as part of their process. You have intergenerational pain when you can "feel" a heaviness or darkness that is somehow bigger than you and you are not able to explain this feeling. Intergenerational pain shows up in resistance to move beyond previously held family accomplishments.

The great news is that intergenerational healing is more powerful than words can describe. I will give it a shot anyway! When you are healing old wounds, no matter the cause, in essence you free your entire generational lineage in all directions and into the future. The transmission, in effect, is stopped and the freeing of the past ignorance is also freed. This is why I can tell children that if they heal their wounds that their parents will also eventually come around and begin to make changes. When one person in the family heals, all are healed. Healing is circular and defies linear understanding.

In our mortal world, we are caught in a linear forward moving sense of time. This is how we, as humans, operate. When an emotional block is cleared and you become free of the block, all aspects of the block are cleared, past, present and future. Because these blocks are energy and energy cannot be destroyed, it can only be changed, the previously stuck energy is now freed. The person feels lighter and all associated, knowingly or unknowingly, are affected and energetically changed.

The story of Elisabeth

Elisabeth is the youngest of 5 children. She has 4 older brothers. She was raised by her parents in a disciplined and often strict family home. Her father, a disciplinarian known for his strict values and demands was the strong paternal figure in the home. Her mother, a creative and intelligent woman, ran the home with precision at the direction of her husband. Elisabeth was a sensitive, creative and somewhat introverted girl. As Elisabeth tells the story; at about age 6, her neighbor boy wanted to be friends. Elisabeth talked him into setting a fire in a neighbor's yard so she could see the fire engines come down the street. Apparently he did it and she became his friend. Her parents never found out that she was behind this event. Elisabeth was mischievous which made for some challenges in her strict family setting.

As Elisabeth grew, she struggled with some of the rigid rules as she was a free spirit at heart. As a late teenage, she met a man who she eventually dated then married. He was conservative and liked her free spirit. Elisabeth and her husband had two children. When asked about parenting, Elisabeth frequently said: "my childhood had far too many harsh rules. You kids will figure out what works for you and do that." Elisabeth allowed her children to set their own rules more and more as they grew. Her oldest child seemed to be somewhat conservative and followed rules well. Her youngest child was a free spirit like her and struggled with the lack of structure and boundaries.

This intergenerational transmission of pain from Elisabeth's childhood was translated as a lack of guidelines for her children. Elisabeth acted in response to her upbringing which gives it the power in the raising of her children. Now, Elisabeth's children will be healing any transmission of pain that was in response to Elisabeth's upbringing. The pain of harsh discipline became the loose boundaries and guidelines that created challenges for her children. In the event Elisabeth's children do not work through the transmission of pain of harsh discipline, then the grandchildren will be dealing with and healing the effects. If they do not then the list goes on. I am sure you get the drift at this point. Whatever is not properly integrated keeps getting passed along. When someone is healing old issues the pain can often feel bigger than the person themselves. This is because of the intergenerational nature of some grief.

Chapter 15

Contentment, Joy and Freedom

It seems that most people start to make life changes because of fear of a problem occurring or getting worse. You may want to change to get an authority or family member off your back. Maybe the changes you seek are coming from within your own being. In order to be successful with making changes, there comes the time when you must move out of fear as your primary motivator and into love or faith as your primary motivator. Ultimately, it is your feelings that you are seeking to experience or avoid. Being afraid of the feelings you do not want to experience will help you get started on your road away from loneliness. This fear alone will not sustain you.

There comes the time when love for yourself and the power of the uplifting feelings you are seeking from the changes must become the motivators. In business circles I have heard this termed as *knowing your why*. The Loneliness Cure is a system that will help you become reconnected and therefore loneliness will not be prevalent in your day to day life. If you are motivated by the fear of being alone or loneliness itself, the cure will work very well initially. The power of the change begins to lose effectiveness if you continue to make changes based on fear.

Work on the emotional aspect of the cure to begin to have love for yourself and all others. After all, you are doing the best you can on any given day with your available resources. When you know better and do not do better it is because that knowledge is not available to you for some reason and you are acting on insufficient understanding. Develop love for you and others. People who are not good to be around can be loved from a distance. No need to keep returning to that empty well or that lion's den for no reason. Turn around and walk forward toward contentment and joy.

Contentment is that state of happiness and ease that you may be wondering if it is even possible for you to feel. Well, not only is contentment possible, it is highly likely the more you are living the loneliness cure by taking daily action. Contentment consists of being happy, satisfied and grateful. Notice that these are real emotions and states of being. Chances are that if you have been lonely for a period of time or the previous methods you attempted haven't sustained, you may be questioning your ability to achieve contentment.

The answer is yes! Of course you can achieve contentment. No one person or group has the monopoly on contentment and no matter how long it has been, you too can regain your sense of satisfaction and gratitude once again. There will be a day shortly after beginning daily action that you will notice contentment. You most likely will identify contentment because of the conspicuous absence of the loneliness, grief and sadness cloud. That absence is not boredom, it is contentment.

Get familiar with this contented and peaceful experience and soon, you will experience authentic joy. This comes after daily action over a period of time. The key word here is authentic. You may be good at faking your happiness or joy to keep others away. I am speaking here about authentic joy that begins at your core and emerges out through your bright eyes and big smile. Joy ushers in increased energy. You will now realize how much energy you had been wasting on fear and loneliness because you are now full of energy and joyful! The Cure keeps working and taking you to new places over time. Remember, there is no finish line.

Even during challenging times, the residual impact of contentment and joy helps ease the struggles. No matter what, keep taking the positive actions. They compound and will help you through any life struggle. As you practice the Cure over time, you will realize you are free. Real freedom will have entered. No longer are you a prisoner or slave to loneliness and the fears surrounding loneliness.

Freedom, you are free despite your skepticism. By developing daily habits you have sprung yourself from the trap of loneliness, isolation and separation. Congratulations! Freedom does not come by wishing for it or thinking about it. Freedom and Joy come by taking action. You must do something focused on your goals. If you are struggling with quitting the bad habits, that is addressed in my previous book *How to Quit Anything in 5 Simple Steps*.

There are times in life when you may fall away from daily action. Distractions are common today and no one lives in complete isolation, unaffected by others. The good news is that you now have in your possession the cure to the problem. You can simply re-read the cure section then start taking action. It won't be long and you will see results beginning once again. If you struggle repeatedly, re-read part one of this book and identify the impact, causes, effects and consequences that you are facing in the pain of the struggle. Become clear on the problem, and then the solution will be even more evident.

Yes, the loneliness cure will lead you out of loneliness and toward contentment, joy and freedom. Yes, you must be the one to take the action. Yes, the results are up to you. Yes, receive assistance, support and encouragement from others. Yes, release what no longer serves you. Yes, use your natural gifts to your benefit. Yes, be willing to receive the good life. You are meant to shine and be magnificent. Now, go for it!

Afterword – Putting It All Together

Loneliness, like contentment is experienced by people every day. You have, I imagine, had many responses to the topic of loneliness and the cure. This book has come to you as a thought provoking vehicle meant to invite you out of loneliness and into a contented life.

Part one examines loneliness and the significant impact it has on each of us personally. Every day the destruction that can be linked to loneliness seems to be increasing. Part two presents the basics of the cure with a summarizing chapter and a diagram for your reference. This is a simple yet relatively challenging model to integrate into daily life. I invite you to study the content and see how it can personally apply to your life. Part three begins the transformation journey.

There is no end point and this plan is designed for ongoing growth. In the event you fall away or neglect parts of the cure, you can easily become re-engaged and you will begin to feel and see results quickly. It is important to me to present a solution that is workable and one that can be used throughout life.

All of the stories are fictional and represent common challenges I see when I read the news or listen to what is happening around. My hope is that you can relate with many of the stories and be inspired to follow the path to your freedom.

By investing a short thirty minutes daily with each of these major life areas, you can transform your life quickly. For those of you who dislike or struggle with delayed gratification, this is the plan for you. Invest in your life, health and welfare and your life will be joy filled in ways beyond your imagination. Thirty minutes each day mentally involves learning something new and examining your self-talk and belief systems. Emotionally, spend your time with self-love or compassion or healing an old wound with forgiveness on some level. Physically, care for your body in a loving manner. Spiritually, develop your connection in the right and perfect way for you. Socially, create and access multiple peer groups. You will soon find that your life is more fulfilling and rewarding.

Variety in your actions is a great idea. Thirty minutes daily does not mean the same thing day in and day out. Give yourself the chance to try new activities, document your experiences and be open to a new, more fulfilled life. *Kaizen* is a Japanese word that speaks to making small changes over time for big results. In our bigger, better, more society; you may want to begin to make the shift to a more compassionate and friendly way of being. Aim for 1% a day and compound this daily. You will see the results, I assure you.

Here are some things to remember:

- Your willingness leads the way to your success!
- Expanding your self-awareness will open you to new possibilities.
- Your words have creative power and they can build up or destroy. It is up to you.
- There is a difference between loneliness and being alone.
- Connection within and without is the correction.
- Your breath can change everything. Breathe deeply for a richer life.
- Practice letting go of what no longer serves you.

- Acceptance of you must be in place in order to truly accept others.
- Smile, laugh and celebrate you!
- For mental clarity, learn something new every day and challenge the untruths in your own thinking. An example is to challenge the "I'm no good" type of self-talk. This simply is not true.
- For emotional freedom, express your feelings in healthy ways. Allow for the flow of your energy without labels and judgment.
- For physical ease, hydrate your body and keep it moving in healthy ways. Breathe!
- For spiritual assurance, spend time each day in quiet reflection, listening to your inner guidance. Connect with nature often.
- For social connection, establish multiple peer groups. Connect humanly with people every day. Electronic methods are not preferable. Human connection is vital for health on every level.
- Be patient, have frequent feedback to be sure you are heading in the direction you choose.
- Always follow your inner, higher guidance while being kind and compassionate toward you and others.

Things change and life is curious with its twists and turns. You have a right to be here and to be part of the great human family. Keep breathing; let the sun warm you and the breeze cool you. The cure to loneliness is at hand and you are the one to take the action. You are wonderful and capable. Reading this book will not immediately realize your goals. It takes focused action in order to have powerful results. Remain open and teachable. Pay attention. Remain focused on your goal, be patient with you.

MEPSS is a powerful cure for the separation and loneliness that you may experience in different ways at different times in your life. This has been an invitation to open up and be willing to take a road not traveled by many in order to spring you from the trap of loneliness. I hope you take the invitation and use it every day. Peace to you.

Conclusion

The Cure in Action: A Case Study

MEPSS, as this way of living has been lovingly termed, has grown out of many years of helping people achieve their personal best. Many have come with varied life challenges including and others seeking a higher quality of life. I first visualized MEPSS unaware of the significance and the long term benefits that would be achieved by so many people over time. The ideas were advanced in comparison to many of the colleagues yet they were natural for me. By sharing a case study along with how these concepts work in practical application, it is my hope that you will be able to identify the use of this system for your life as well as your loved ones. Carlos is a fictional character that comprises many common challenges that MEPSS can be used to offer viable solutions to cure loneliness and regain a sense of connection.

Carlos has always been a visionary and someone who could create, establish and maintain powerful systems for corporate use. For many years, Carlos was naïve to these gifts, rather he thought all people possessed the same gifts and they weren't using them. When people would share their amazement or awe about his gifts, he was gracious yet internally he questioned their perceptions and his experiences. As time has unfolded, Carlos came to know and use these gifts and has allowed them to emerge more each day.

During his career and professional life, Carlos excelled in creating systems to assist coworkers and others in work productivity. He even was the designated trainer for new hires. This was a gift that was once revealed to Carlos by a friend who stated "You can teach a topic to someone that they don't want to learn and they will learn it and be successful in spite of their best efforts to fail." He was thinking that he had no "teaching ability" until his friend said something His friend was gifted at teaching and education activities so Carlos could hear this feedback in an entirely different way than others. Carlos is naturally introverted and this has been misunderstood by many throughout his life. He has been called cold, aloof, distant and weird to name a few. As he grew personally, he began to see these gifts and his need to be alone to re-charge as an asset, not a liability. Until he was able to embrace this part of his life, he struggled with relationships and self-esteem. When Carlos was feeling down or lonely, he would isolate making things worse. When he would finally surface, he found himself feeling embarrassed in the company of others for no real reason.

Carlos decided to retire from his career as it was too demanding and draining and he was suffering personally. He took a year off and did some side jobs and relaxed. He was not willing to be unhappy any longer and at a price that was too high. During that year he prayed, meditated, cleaned out clutter, learned new things, ate healthfully and worked out. Daily, he took care of himself and his personal priorities. It wasn't long and he was on top of the world and alive in ways spiritually and physically like never before. He went from exhausted and worn down to alive and passionate once again about life and his career. "Thank God" he said every day. Every night he asked to be of service and be a positive influence and each day he had the chance to realize his visions.

The main challenge for Carlos was how to keep this feeling and way of living alive while working full time as his self-care and spiritual development was his full time job so to speak. He was not aware that he had the answer already in his life. He began to create a spiritually principled company with another seemingly spiritually principled person he had met through a trusted friend. Their first meeting inspired Carlos to begin to create once again for others. In short order, this new endeavor was moving forward. The two men spoke daily and began to work toward the vision. Carlos was working part time at a job that was easy and almost entertaining while continuing the MEPSS way of life with little interruption until this time. He noticed his work load increasing with his new project and his part time job but then again creating and putting together progressive concepts was exhilarating for Carlos. He remembered what it was like to allow his creativity to express. The connection Carlos had made with a dynamic, like minded person was meeting other areas of MEPSS so his investment of time and talent seemed to be working.

Carlos and his partner's new venture opened and Carlos' time was now allotted primarily to this venture and the people involved with it. Carlos enjoyed the success of seeing his vision and creation coming into reality. It didn't feel like work for Carlos because it was his vision. Slowly, Carlos stopped working out and he became a workhorse for the company. He was happy to do the extra work because he *knew* he and his partner were building a great company. Carlos kept his spiritual life active; doing what he believed was his duty. Slowly, he drifted away from what was keeping him emotionally and physically content and joyful. His life was getting off balance. Carlos knew this yet kept saying: "this is a sacrifice worth making and that it was temporary and we all have seasons in our lives".

Carlos kept making excuses for his own inaction and also for the inaction of others.

As time progressed, though, he began having fewer happy days and more days of frustration. He needed help at work as he was the go to person who had learned the guidelines for the new company and how to negotiate the system. Carlos had progressive amounts of pressure internally and externally to keep things going well and to educate others about the processes. He was successful and the new company was growing and it began to take an even bigger toll on Carlos' health and relationships. Carlos realized he was not following his new life of MEPSS real well so he attempted to talk to a few people at church who were judgmental and seemed not to understand. Carlos closed up more and the stress and lack of outlet and fulfillment outside of work started showing in his attitude and interactions. There were days that he simply couldn't help from yelling when no one was looking. Carlos was frustrated wondering what has happened to his "friends" and "confidants". He needed a release and someone to talk to that was outside of his corporate life. The days of feeling intense gratitude for the new company were gone. He was grateful but feeling the overwhelming sense of gratitude was gone. Carlos and his partner began to distance from each other. The price of growing pains, Carlos imagined.

For several months, Carlos' world was punctuated by work and divisions among he and the co-workers that seemed to be challenging in ways he had never experienced. The struggle was daily and which way to focus seemed clouded by personalities, perceptions and the regular pace of working long hours. Carlos was simply too busy to give credence to the misguided and seemingly malicious behavior around him. Sadly the majority of discord was within the ranks of employees. Things were changing around him and he did not see the changes happening. Carlos was struggling much like many corporate men who give everything to their work and become like machines then begin to struggle with life equilibrium.

Carlos finally took a week vacation to rest. By the second day, he could see the situation clearly. He was beaten down and he was second guessing himself; unsure if anyone believed in him any longer. He decided to speak with his business partner. Initially, the conversation was focused on "Carlos' problem". This is the time when good listening and open mindedness are vital in any relationship.

Back to work, still doing the work of several people, Carlos was tired before long. He resumed his workout schedule and began to talk to friends again. This was important as Carlos could see how out of alignment he had gotten, all trying to do his best. Carlos was so confused. He had a solution he had been practicing yet it was so hard to follow through. Still MEPSS was not in balance and he was attempting to regain the equilibrium that he had known in his recent life.

The cycle continues and Carlos feels himself becoming less tolerant of re-doing work and correcting messes of others. He is sleeping less and struggling with concentration. He was able to do his basic tasks and he was getting by everywhere else. His personal work responsibilities suffered as he was ensuring that everyone else's things were done. Carlos struggled with health issues and sought outside medical care to help with stress related problems. As he felt better, he could more clearly see the problems he was dealing with in regard to being out of balance. Still, Carlos struggled with regaining his alignment. He realized this time that thinking about doing the action and actually doing the action were very different when it came to outcome.

Several months later, Carlos takes another short vacation following verbal violence targeted at Carlos in the workplace. Carlos was trying to make sense of this situation only exacerbated his frustration and pain. He distanced himself from nearly everyone at work. It was a very sad day for Carlos. What was coming of this great company? Friends would inquire and Carlos was at a loss for words. Carlos opted for general responses and then changing the subject. Carlos had a few close spiritual friends who assisted him with making changes and realigning his life and his work.

Carlos worked on regaining his physical balance and health. He had to reduce his stress and exercise to correct muscle tightness and pain from tension. Carlos worked with people who helped with nutrition, exercise and his physical environment. He also pulled out his MEPSS paperwork and began to take an inventory so he could get back on track. Carlos made small changes in each of the five areas daily. Slowly, Carlos began to smile. He eventually laughed again.

As a result of Carlos' willingness to take action and focus on his vision to create amazing companies, he now works toward creating a balanced work experience. Carlos learned his lesson about not using his discernment when meeting someone, even if a trusted person introduced did the introduction. Carlos has made changes and he shared recently with me that he uses MEPSS everyday now and doesn't let work or fears of his own value get in the way. It was nice to hear him laugh again.

The beauty of this MEPSS model is that you can start anytime from any place. It works no matter what limited time you may have initially. Loneliness blocks your clarity and often you cannot see opportunities that are being presented. MEPSS is ever expanding and can always serve you and your life. Just as Carlos did, you too can pull out information and begin from the place you are, no matter what. Your previous lessons and successes are always with you. Any self-defeating mind games can be out aside and you can take daily action toward your personal contentment, joy and freedom.

Glossary

Many times the operational use of words can vary from the literal or dictionary definition. Below are some words I have used in the text with the operational definition that best applies to this writing.

Alone – To be physically without another in close physical proximity

Assurance – To have a guarantee, promise or commitment

Comparative Model of Transformation – MEPSS model that is the basis for *The Loneliness Cure*

Contentment – To be happy, satisfied and grateful

Ease – To be in the flow of life

Enoughness – Being worthy and feeling as if you are enough just the way you are

Freedom – Liberation from the bindings of limitations that had previously held you back

Guilt – The feeling you experience when you break your own rules or cross your own boundary.

Joy – Energetic excitement that comes from within

Kaizen – To do small things daily to yield solid long term results

Loneliness – To be disconnected from one's purpose and Source

MEPSS- Mental, Emotional, Physical, Spiritual, Social model for living

MPG – Multiple Peer Group

Peers – Like-minded people sharing common beliefs within a certain group

People Picker – The part of you that chooses to associate with or trust

Shame – The belief that you are unworthy and have no value as a person

Spiritual – Root means "to be set free". Being connected to your life's purpose and calling. Freedom arises from this connection.

Synergy – The interaction of two or more forces so that their combined effect is greater than the sum of the individual forces.

About Dianne A. Allen, MA

Catalyst, free thinker, mentor, ambassador, motivator, visionary are all words used to describe Dianne A. Allen, MA. Her powerful writing comes as part of her many years of listening and assisting others with sorting out their life challenges. Dianne's education, experience and inspiration give her unique perspectives that she shares in her writing and speaking engagements. Dianne holds a Bachelor's Degree in Psychology and a Master's Degree in Rehabilitation Counseling. She has studied formally and informally throughout her adult life. She offers authentic and strategic solutions. Dianne lives in Tampa Bay, Florida and currently mentors corporate leaders and business owners in applying their visions with focused action. Dianne is an ambassador for bright and talented individuals and families, speaking at SENG's (Supporting Emotional Needs of Gifted) International Conference annually. She is the author of *How to Quit Anything in 5 Simple Steps*.

Visit her website: www.visionsapplied.com

CPSIA information can be obtained at www.ICGtesting.com
Printed in the USA
LVOW12s0034031214

416766LV00002B/4/P